Life 3.0

Protirement NOT Retirement

Ellis Katsof, MSW

MyProtirement

Walter
Happy Protirement
Planning!
Ellis

Published by: *My*Protirement

*My*Protirement, St. Catharines,
Ontario, Canada

First published: 2017

Cover design by: Steve Nease

LIBRARY AND ARCHIVES CANADA CATALOGUING IN PUBLICTION

Katsof, Ellis, 1951 Oct. 14-
Life 3.0
ISBN 978-0-9959306-2-9 (Book)

ISBN 978-0-9959306-3-6 (Digital)

For my wife, Coletta, whose ongoing support, encouragement
and creative input helped make this book a reality;
and for my children,
Devan, Brynne, and Zachary,
whose pursuit of their life passions
have been wonderful models for me during this journey.

ACKNOWLEDGEMENT

I would like to thank all the amazing people who allowed me to interview them for this book. Whether their individual stories ended up in the book or not, they added so much to my understanding of people's experiences during the protirement process. I am extremely grateful to everyone for being so open and honest with me about their own experiences. I would also like to thank Rosemarie Perla for introducing me to the "Protirement" concept, which began my exploration of life after retirement for Boomers. As well, I have to thank Alex Digenis for encouraging me to write the book when, at the outset of this journey, I was wavering; and for his honest challenges throughout the journey. The final product is as much a result of my research and writing as it is of my editor, Danica. Thank you for your professional and creative editing. Thanks to Steve Crane for your creative concept for the cover, and to Steve Nease for bringing that concept to life. And finally, thank you to everyone on social media who has expressed an interest in the book, your interest and encouragement has been wonderful.

TABLE OF CONTENTS

INTRODUCTION

"You never change something by fighting the existing reality. To change something, build a new model that makes the existing model obsolete."
Buckminster Fuller

In October 2016, I turned 64. I had always planned on working until I was 70, but over the last couple of years, my social work career grew tedious and challenging. I loved my 40-year career. Unfortunately, changes in government policy began affecting how much I enjoyed my work.

I was always positive about work, even when social services experienced tough times during economic down turns. But this was different. I was concerned that it would have an impact on how I viewed the course of my entire career, not just the conclusion of my career. In December 2016, I took the plunge, along with many other Baby Boomers, and decided to retire. My last day at work was January 15, 2017.

A week after my retirement, I attended the annual Mayor's Luncheon. Typically, people arrive early to network before the luncheon begins. As CEO of a large social service agency and its foundation, this type of networking event was an important part of my job and one I enjoyed. The networking was important to our fund raising efforts. I enjoyed working the room, meeting people, introducing myself, learning more about others, and making new contacts.

Strangely, this year, the experience was different. Suddenly, people were coming up to me, introducing themselves, giving me business cards, and asking who I was. I panicked. I found myself reaching for non-existent business cards, because I had just retired. Who was I? Who did I work for? What was my identity? How did I introduce myself? All the things that related to my job, my career, my self-identity, were no longer relevant.

I left the luncheon and quickly realized I was not prepared for this sudden change in life. I decided to start a management consulting firm. Since I had been a partner in a consulting firm in the mid 1990s, it was easy to do. I was confident in my skills and had a 40 year reputation in Ontario to build upon. Since I was not ready to retire and hang out at home, and was also concerned that my retirement savings might not last if I was fortunate to live another 20 or 30 years, this would meet a number of needs. It would provide me with a new professional identity and would also supplement my retirement income.

I did not realize how bored I'd become. As a management consultant, I was doing similar work to what I had done for many years. I was ready for a real change but not sure what that meant. After thinking about all the different things that I had done in my career, I realized two things. First, my personal career mission, developed with the help of Rosemarie Perla, a personal coach in 2007, was to be a change agent and to help thousands of people positively improve their lives. Second, I really enjoyed public speaking. Since I knew it was important to talk about things that are relevant in your life, I decided to launch a public speaking career focused on changing people's attitudes toward retirement.

As I was sorting out what retirement meant to me, I decided to do some research into how Baby Boomers were retiring. I quickly found that there was little written about the topic; 95% of the retirement books were about financial planning rather than retirement lifestyles. I visited a friend, Alex Digenis, and was excited to tell him about my new business plan. Alex, always supportive, is also the first one to build on your ideas. His first comment was, "Ellis, you need to write a book to base your keynote speeches on. It will give you more credibility as a speaker." I thought about it and realized he was right. I decided to interview 10 or 15 colleagues who had retired, and then self-publish a small book on their experiences.

After the first 10 interviews, I was hooked. The stories were so rich and wonderful that I couldn't stop at 10. I interviewed 10 more, and then 10 more. I realized I needed to interview people from all walks of life, and began asking those I interviewed if they knew anyone who'd be interested in being part of my book. Before I knew it, I had interviewed people from varied backgrounds, including: bankers, teachers, automotive workers, financial analysts, doctors, lawyers, musicians, secretaries, a coal miner, a fire fighter, politicians, psychologists, management consultants, tin smiths, small business owners, and corporate CEO's.

I interviewed Baby Boomers and pre-Baby Boomers, and patterns began to emerge in their post-retirement activities. I became curious about whether these patterns would be similar for well-known Canadians, too. I began contacting some to see if they would be interested in being interviewed. I found that people were more than willing to share their personal stories. I was fortunate to interview people like Ronnie Hawkins, Lloyd Robertson, Liona Boyd, Ken Dryden, and Terry O'Reilly.

A publisher suggested that I interview some Americans, as well. Included in my American interviews are people like a former Governor of Pennsylvania, the first Secretary for Homeland Security, Tom Ridge, former Apple CEO, Gil Amelio, current Yahoo CFO, Ken Goldman, and Dr. George Wood, the current Chairman of the Assembly of God (the largest evangelical church in the world).

Before I realized it, I had interviewed over 100 people, taking down enough stories to fill several books. I put on my researcher hat, developed through years of consulting work and writing policy papers for regional and provincial governments, and began to analyze the stories, looking for trends. Clear patterns emerged. First, and most importantly, Baby Boomers felt and acted very differently about "retirement" than previous generations. They dreaded the concept of being "retired" and were scared of being treated like they are "retired from life" or "over the hill," as was the feeling of earlier generations. Our early models for retirement were our grandparents. They usually worked until they could no longer work and were fortunate if they had five years of life post-retirement. They led very quiet retirement lives.

Our generation has benefited from increased health promotion and health care. With robust pension plans, we can also retire at a younger age than our grandparents. We will live much longer that they did. It is highly likely that Baby Boomers will live an additional 20 or 30 years beyond retirement. It is possible that the third chapter of our lives could be as long as our working years. We could easily live a third of our lives in "retirement."

Baby Boomers are not ready to stop living. We have a strong desire to keep active, be productive, and stay engaged in life. Many boomers also have a need to continue earning money because they do not have sufficient savings to lead the lives they would like to have in retirement. The stock market crash of 2008 had a major impact on the retirement savings of many Baby Boomers.

Baby Boomers no longer see retirement as a destination. It has now become step one in a journey. My analysis identified that Baby Boomers are going through a three-stage process, similar to William Bridges *Transition Theory of Change*. The first stage is the "Retirement Phase." The second stage is the, "Transition Zone," and the third stage is the, "Protirement Stage." The Protirement Stage is where we pursue fulfilling activities.

I identified 17 different Protirement activity categories Baby Boomers are embracing. I was intrigued to find that many Baby Boomers are working during their Protirement. Four of the 17 Protirement Categories refer to different types of work. The remaining 13 Protirement Categories are non-income generating activities.

The following chapters will: 1) provide you with an historical overview of retirement; 2) describe the transition process and how we move from retirement to Protirement; and 3) introduce the Protirement Checkerboard with the 17 Protirement Categories. Each Protirement Category will be described using relevant research and personal stories from the people who were interviewed.

I will also share the "advice" people gave during the interviews, explaining how they think others can have an easier transition from retirement to Protirement. Using this advice, people can develop their own individualized Protirement Lifestyle Plans.

CHAPTER 1.
THE EVOLUTION OF PENSIONS AND RETIREMENT

"Nothing is more usual than the sight of old people who yearn for retirement, and nothing is so rare than those who have retired and do not regret it."
Charles de Saint-Evermond

The History of Retirement & Pensions

The first government sponsored pension plan began in 1889 in Prussia. Chancellor Bismarck introduced the Old Age Pension for workers 70 years and older. Although it was a novel plan, the average life span at the time was only 52, so few Prussians were able to take advantage of the pension. The next Chancellor, Leo von Caprivi, lowered the starting age to 65.

Private pension plans began in the USA with the American Express Company in 1875. By 1919, there were over 300 private pension plans, covering about 15% of the American working population. In the late 1800s, private pension plans also began in Canada, mostly with industries like the railroads.

In 1927, the Canadian government enacted the first federal Old Age Pensions Act to support the poorest seniors in Canada. In 1935, the USA enacted the Social Security Act and set the retirement age at 65. In 1951, Canada enacted the Old Age Security Act, which provided a universal pension to all Canadians, aged 70 and older. At the same time, Canada introduced the Old

Age Assistance Act, which provided a means-tested pension to retired Canadians between the ages of 65 and 69. In 1965, Canada enacted the Canadian Pension Plan, a compulsory plan to which both employers and employees contributed.

In the late 1800s, most North American seniors worked on the family farm, in local factories, or small businesses. In addition to relying on personal savings, they usually passed on the family farm or business to their children, who in turn supported them during their retirement.

In the 1950s, when Baby Boomers were being born, retirement for their grandparents was very simple and modest; it wasn't seen as the golden years. Recreational air travel had not yet begun and air fare was expensive. Hardly anyone ate at restaurants, played golf, or took recreational cruises. The average number of years between retirement and death was only about eight years. They didn't know that many illnesses like heart disease and diabetes were largely caused by poor lifestyle choices; smoking was still an accepted practice. After retirement, this generation spent time focusing on family, friends, community, and church.

For our grandparents, the decision to retire was a major one; from working one day to not working the next. Some people describe the change as so abrupt that it was like coming to a cliff edge and jumping. Baby Boomers' parents began living fuller lives during their retirement, but retirement still meant the end of full-time employment and the beginning of a quieter, simpler life. Think about it. The retirement concept had only begun changing, modestly, one generation before the baby boom generation. Our parents began joining retirement communities as they sprouted up in warmer climates like Florida and Arizona. Time shares, golf courses, inexpensive cruises, and recreational air travel were also part of the new retirement scene. Although life expectancy was beginning to grow for this generation, major gains were only to occur for *our* generation, the Baby Boomers. Our parents still only expected to live about 15 years beyond retirement, whereas we can expect to live another 25 or 30 years beyond our retirement, almost a another third of our lives.

Current Times

In 1989, the insurance industry launched the first ad promoting the Freedom 55 concept. At that time, the youngest Baby Boomers were 43. The investment goal was to build retirement funds so you could retire when you turned 55. Fast forward to 2008, and 51% of Canadian workers over the age of 30, according to a Sun Life Financial survey, believed they would be fully retired by the age of 66. In 2013, after the 2008 economic crisis, only 27% expected to be fully retired by the age of 66[1]. This trend has continued, not only for economic reasons but also for personal reasons.

Throughout their lives, the baby boom generation have been cultural change agents. They are known as the "counter culture generation." They were influenced by the Civil Rights movement, the feminist movement, the Vietnam War protests, the Cold War, the assassinations of JFK, Robert Kennedy and Martin Luther King, the Cuban Missile Crisis, Beatlemania, Woodstock, the October Crisis, Trudeaumania, the first walk on the moon, the sexual freedom movement, and more. Being the first generation to grow up with television, they were also the first generation to be exposed to mass advertising, and were known as the "Me" generation because of their consumerism.

Baby Boomers were the first generation to have personal devices like transistor radios, which allowed them to listen to their music wherever they were, without electrical outlets. They were the first generation to grow up with televisions (my kids can't believe this and laugh when reminded about it) and grew up watching the Mickey Mouse Club, Brady Bunch, Gilligan's Island, Bonanza, the Ed Sullivan Show, All in the Family, and Happy Days.

Baby Boomers were known for their experimentation, individualism, challenging of the norms, social cause orientation, and free spiritedness. They had such an impact on society that in 1966, *Time Magazine* named the baby boom generation as the "Man of the Year."

It is no wonder that Baby Boomers have chosen not to sit back and just accept past retirement practices. In the interviews I conducted, I found Baby Boomers consistently challenging old retirement practices for many reasons.

First, life spans for Baby Boomers have grown, thanks to significantly improved medical practices, health promotion campaigns, and healthy lifestyle choices. As a result, Baby Boomers can expect to live 20, 25, or 30 years beyond retirement. This is a long time to just sit around and "retire from life."

Second, Baby Boomers dislike the stigma related to being "retired." They feel as though people treat them differently once they know they're retired. After they retire, the status and prestige related to their job quickly disappears. My interviews were filled with quotes about ageism and the stigma related to retirement.

Baby Boomers see themselves as energetic, young, and engaged in life; just the opposite of what "retired" means. Numerous people have said, "75 is the new 65," and the concept of 'retirement' is outdated.

Third, many Baby Boomers are concerned that their retirement savings will be insufficient. The economic crisis of 2008 had a significant negative impact on retirement savings for Boomers. Also, few retirement savings plans accounted for the fact that people would depend on their retirement savings for 30 years or more, or the potentially expensive nursing home and/or long term care arrangements.

Baby Boomers clearly wanted to spend their retirement years as active individuals, and wanted to be respected and appreciated as people who have something to offer to others, no matter what their age.

Yes, Baby Boomers have changed how they retire, what they are doing, and how they are perceived in their later lives. After retirement, Boomers want to live fulfilling, active, meaningful lives.

When I first retired, a good friend and former coach, Rosemarie Perla, emailed me, telling me she didn't believe I was retiring, that it wasn't in my DNA to 'retire' from life, so what was I really planning on doing after I retired from my career? She suggested that I look up the word "Protirement." Being an excellent coach, Rosemarie always had provocative questions at just the right time.

I was curious, so I looked up the word. The word 'Protirement' was first recorded in the *American Mercury* in January 1961, and was attributed to Arthur Godfrey[2]. At that time, it was defined as: "Early retirement from professional work with the positive idea of pursuing something more fulfilling." Dictionary.com explains that the origin came from combining parts of two words: **pro** active + re **tirement** to create **Protirement.**

Buckminster Fuller, a futurist, believed that great inventions were often created 50 years ahead of their adoption. I believe this the case for 'Protirement'. The word has only taken on serious meaning within the circles of aging Baby Boomers. The first countries to purposefully adopt use of the word 'Protirement' were Australia and the UK in 2010. Although there is limited use of the word in Canada or the US, it is only a matter of time before we all begin using it, as well. It is relevant to the four million North Americans per year, until 2030, who are turning 65. Everyone I interviewed loved the term and felt it better reflected their post retirement lifestyle than the word "retired."

"Protirement" rings a chord, not only with Baby Boomers, but also with anyone of retirement age. It is applicable to everyone, whether you have chosen to retire or to work into your later years. I have tweaked the definition to mean: "The pursuit of fulfilling activities in the third chapter of our lives, whether we chose to retire or not."

A New Paradigm

The old paradigm of aging, for previous generations, had three stages of life, beginning with Childhood/Adolescence from birth to 21, then moving into Adulthood at age 21, and ending with Old Age and Retirement, beginning at age 65. Life spans lasted into our early or mid 70s, and life after retirement was slow paced.

Old Paradigm:

Birth – 21	21 – 65	65 – 75
Childhood Adolescence	Adulthood	Old Age
		Retirement

As Baby Boomers aged, their outlook on life changed, and the Old Paradigm gave way to a new Paradigm. George Burns summarized this change perfectly when he said: "You can't help getting older, but you don't have to get old."

I describe the New Paradigm in the following way:

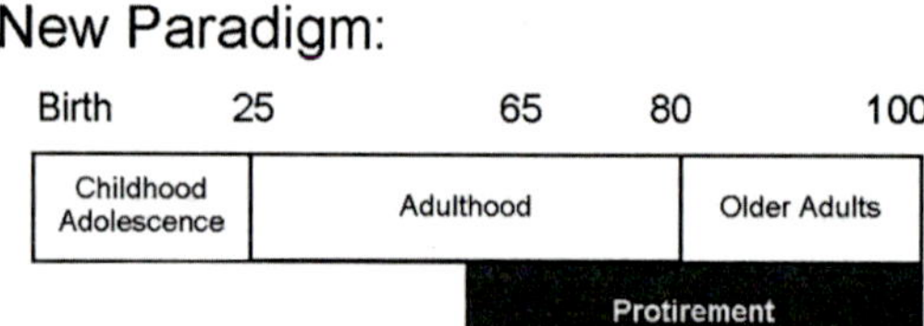

The Childhood/Adolescence stage has extended to age 25. Because Boomers have experienced significant improvements in their health, the Adulthood stage has now extended to age 80. Some people may argue that it only extends to age 75, but after interviewing 100 people, many in their 70s and 80s, I chose 80 as the transition into Older Adulthood.

Old Age is a stigmatizing term and clearly does not reflect everyone over 80 years old. A more appropriate term for this age group is 'Older Adults'. As people age, their health begins to deteriorate and their level of disability increases. Active adults tend to remain active Older Adults, the only difference is often a decrease in the level of activity. As Boomers age and move into their Older Adulthood, they'll still enjoy the same activities, they just won't do them as often. This varies from individual to individual and will depend more on health and ability/disability than on age.

Protirement begins when an individual retires from their main employment, which occurs for most Boomers between the ages of 50 and 65. Some of these Boomers choose to pursue other types of work *after* they retire, but they also pursue other types of non-work Protirement activities. Others are continuing to work after the age of 65 and are not retiring from their jobs, but rather enjoying non-work related activities.

Health is a major indicator of how active a protired individual will be. Harold, an 86 year old protired men's wear store owner, is a wonderful example of an active protiree. He still works three days a week at the family store, which is now operated by his son, the third generation. He is president of a local synagogue, plays bridge at the local bridge club three or four times a week, and, until a few years ago, played tennis a few times a week. He was a regular member of a local Rotary Club until recently, when he retired his long-term membership, becoming an honorary member.

Harold is an exemplary "Older Adult" rather than someone in their "Old Age."

Pam, an 86-year-old retired secretary, spends her days as a champion of heritage buildings. She is still an active part of her local heritage committee and provides advice to heritage groups throughout the province. Active into her 80s, she has won awards acknowledging her work saving heritage buildings. In 2016, she was honored with the Woman of the Year Award from the Greater Niagara Chamber of Commerce. In 2011, she received the George and Olive Seibel Award for outstanding contribution to the preservation of the history of Niagara. In 2002, she was honored with the Queen's Golden Jubilee Medal. Pam's favorite quote is: "If you believe it, and can commit to it, *do it*!"

The following chapters describe Protirement through the eyes of the 100 North Americans interviewed for this book.

CHAPTER 2:
BABY BOOMERS: TRANSITIONING FROM RETIREMENT TO PROTIREMENT

"For those of you who don't know what to do after retirement, the answer is easy: Transition to Protirement, and do what you really want to do!"
Ellis Katsof

During the research phase of this project, I decided to interview some well-known individuals to see if their stories varied in any way from the others. I interviewed people like the Ronnie Hawkins, Lloyd Robertson, Gil Amelio, and the Honourable Tom Ridge. Interestingly, their post-retirement stories were very similar to everyone else's.

During the interviews, I asked each person five questions and allowed them to tell me their individual stories in their own words. First, I asked them to tell me about their 'Work Story', from when they began working to when they retired (or up to present, since some of them aren't retired, even though they were older than 65). Second, I asked them to tell me about their 'life outside of work', including time spent with family, hobbies, community, faith groups, etc. Third, if they had retired, I asked them to talk about the period just before and after they retired, and to share with me any challenges they experienced. Fourth, I asked them to talk to me about their retirement experience, including their activities, how they felt about being retired, etc. Lastly, I asked them what advice they would give others to make their retirement/protirement process easier and enjoyable.

Everyone was forthcoming and enjoyed the opportunity to review their lives through this window of exploration. Once I had completed the interviews, I analyzed the stories for similarities or trends. I found that the retirement process has evolved throughout the generations. Retirement is no longer a 'destination' but rather one step in the process to "Protirement." Since the Boomer generation is living longer than any previous generation, with the possibility of living a third of their lives after retirement, a change in the way they are responding to retirement has occurred. The change process described in William Bridges book, *Managing Transitions*[3] (first published in 1991), describes the Boomer's retirement process well. I have adapted Bridges 'Transitions' theory to reflect the changes that Boomers are experiencing as they transition from retirement to Protirement.

The change process, as experienced by Baby Boomers, involves three Stages, beginning with the decision to retire and ending with an active new Protirement lifestyle that encompasses the third chapter of Boomers' lives. The three stages are outlined below.

Stage 1: Retirement

Bridges explains that change is external to us, one that we don't have control over, such as a job layoff. Following an external change, we encounter a psychological transition process that is internal and within our control. Using the job layoff example, we can control how we respond to the job layoff. Therefore, he talks about managing Transitions, and not Change.

The first stage of transition, in relation to retirement, is when we decide to retire, or have that decision made for us. Change inevitably means that we have to give up something we're familiar with. In this case, we are faced with giving up a lifetime of work, a career, a profession, along with the daily routines, social status, and personal identity that are connected with our work. Although we have little control over the actual retirement, we do have control over the internal psychological transition we experience once the decision to retire is made. This is often more impactful than the actual retirement.

Stage 1, the Retirement Stage, can be filled with a sense of sadness related to giving up a job or career that was important to us, and/or a sense of excitement about new Protirement activities. Rosemary, a retired Dean of Arts, explained her feeling of sadness in the following way:

"The last few years of my job as Dean were largely focused on opening up a new School of Fine and Performing Arts, working with the city on the Performing Arts Centre and seeing the Faculty of Humanities flourish. All very exciting. The Marilyn I. Walker School of Fine and Performing Arts would open just as I was getting ready to retire. I went to the ground breaking and found myself weeping, tears of both joy and loss." She explained that she was overjoyed at the opening of the new Arts building but she also realized she no longer had her old identity of being a 'Dean'. She wasn't sure who she was any longer. She was extremely sad that this part of her life was coming to an end.

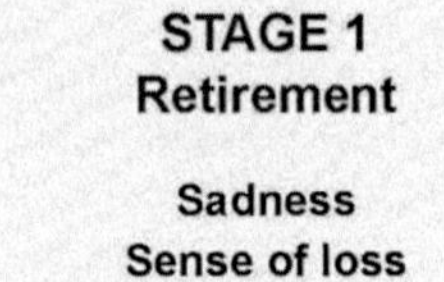

Not everyone is sad. Susan, a retired government administrator, explained her experience as follows:

"My self-worth was never wrapped around work, so that's probably why I don't miss the actual work. I don't feel like I have lost any brain power or anything. I feel the same, just less tired."

Uncertainty is often part of this stage, including uncertainty of what tomorrow morning—the first day after you retire—brings due to a loss of daily work routines and what comes next in your life. John, a retired investment manager, described the uncertainty as: "Suddenly, when I retired, I had nowhere to go in the morning." The uncertainty for John was very challenging.

Ken Dryden, a former NHL hockey player, talked about retirement beginning, not the day of your retirement party, but the first Monday after you retire, when all of your colleagues are going back to work after the weekend and you wake up with nothing to do and nowhere to go. Ken said, "Well, when I retired from the hockey season, I didn't retire in July; I retired in September when training camp began. I was quite overwhelmed by the depth of the feeling I felt in September. It was…'Ah-ha, right, that's what this is'. I had that deep hole in my stomach in September, not in July."

For some, especially those who embrace change more easily than others, a sense of excitement can also be part of this stage. Excitement comes with knowing that when one door closes another always opens, as long as you are willing to look for it and take advantage of the new opportunities. Marty, a retired publisher, was excited about his retirement. He told me: "When I retired, we bought a diesel Volkswagen Golf and planned to take road trips because we loved driving to see new places."

Bridges stressed that the stages aren't distinct from one another. They tend to overlap. Therefore, as we deal with Stage 1 experiences, we may be dealing with some Stage 2 issues, as well.

Stage 2: Transition Zone

In Stage 2, the Transition Zone, Boomers are faced with a range of new experiences.

STAGE 2
Transition Zone

Lack of routine
Loss of social status
Loss of identity
Loss of socializing
Relationship stress
Transition projects
Personal inventory

Lack of Routine

The first day after our retirement party, when we wake up, we are immediately faced with a lack of our daily work-related routines. Can you imagine, waking up and not knowing what to do first? Steve, a retired Rabbi, described his lack of routines thusly:

"Some of the challenges at the beginning of retiring included going from having a very busy schedule to having no schedule. I think that's the hardest thing, you don't have a schedule so you set your own schedule."

Mike, a retired regional government CAO, told me an embarrassing story about routines. "My administrative assistant was always good about taking care of me, making sure that my day was fully scheduled. She managed my calendar. If I tried to do anything with my schedule, I got in trouble with her. Suddenly, I didn't have her to structure my day, but I still had commitments that I suddenly had to schedule myself. The first year after I retired, the United Way kick-off breakfast was in September. I was on the board and they mentioned that it was on September 12th. That was easy to remember because it was my birthday. I totally forgot about it. I didn't have it in my calendar and two days later I had to call the Executive Director and apologize. I had to learn to manage my own calendar and make sure I had stuff written down."

John, a 64-year-old retired government executive, talked to me about how a sudden change in his routine resulted in a challenging bout of depression. "That fall, I was doing theatre and was president of the theatre organization. Around Christmastime, I became depressed. It was something new; I had never experienced that before. My wife is a psychiatric nurse and she knew what it was right away, but I was totally taken aback by it. Looking back, I realize it was, more than anything, because I had just stopped doing anything physical. I wasn't a member of a gym, which was something I'd always done. I hadn't taken up any other interests.

"I was very fortunate that my wife was there. We went to my doctor and worked it through. It took me a while, but once we figured out what it was, I came to grips with it and got the help I needed. I realized that I had to be physically active. I joined the gym and went regularly. I walked, and when golf season returned, I began playing again. When I was depressed, I canceled everything I'd planned to do. That was hard, but my wife helped me back out of all of it. I just rested, rejuvenated, and dealt with all the issues."

Loss of Social Status

Loss of social status is common after retirement. Greg, a corporate CEO, shared a humourous story related to loss of status. "I had a lot of friends in the company and the industry. It's definitely harder to keep in contact. I miss that. We play hockey every Friday morning, so I still see a lot of the guys I know and it keeps me linked to work friends. In hockey, when they knock me down now, they don't pick me up as they did when I was CEO. That's the only difference."

Terry O'Reilly, a 57-year-old retired advertising executive, talked about his concern related to retiring. "I worried about losing my power base in the advertising business, leaving it when I sold my radio and television production company at the age of 53. I worried because a power base is important. I could pick up the phone and call a creative director and get a favor. I worried but it was an unnecessary worry. It's been almost four years now, I've been away from Pirate and advertising, but my power base really hasn't diminished. I think the radio show is a great part of that, because they listen to the show, and know I'm still in the business. When I pick up the phone to call, they're still as responsive as they ever were."

Sandra, a 55-year-old retired Canadian military, held numerous challenging positions in the military, including: executive assistant to a British and Canadian General in Kandahar, Afghanistan. After a very successful military career, she took a part-time job in her retirement to keep busy and fill in the time between missionary trips to South America. Sandra described the change in her social status:

"I am now working part-time as a receptionist for a chiropractor. When you talk about status, it is funny how there are some people who judge you because they see you sitting behind a desk being a receptionist. I really like the job, though, and there are also wonderful people that come into the office and don't judge me."

Loss of Identity

Loss of identity is also a common experience during Stage 2. David, an 82-year-old retired social worker, described his concern about a lack of identity and meaning in life in the following way:

"We need to have a reason for getting up in the morning. Thinking that every day for the rest of your life you are going to be sitting around doing absolutely nothing is very scary. I still, to this day, get cabin fever if I sit in the apartment too long. In the old days, when you retired, you *did* retire. My father and my wife's father just sat down and rocked in their chairs. Their life span after retirement wasn't very long, but I believe it could have been longer if they went on doing something."

Mike, a retired CAO, described his experience in the following way:

"I liked the recognition but didn't have a real hunger for it or for the individual profile that came with the job. I had to get used to it, people giving me the attention because I was in a certain role. It made it easier for me during the transition period. So many people I talked to, who had retired, found—I call it—the relevance phase. They needed to be relevant. For some people, it was the profile and attention that filled this need. I can remember one of them saying, 'It is amazing how quickly people forget you!' So, that's something I think everybody needs to watch out for."

Relationship Stress

Another change that often occurs in the Transition Zone is a change in family relationships. When you retire, if you are in a relationship, your partner will either be working or will have already retired. If your partner is still working, early in your retirement you may find yourself wishing they weren't so they could keep you company and do things with you. If your partner had already retired, they may be busy and not around for you, which can also cause resentment. The first time I shared this insight during a speaking engagement, many people in the audience laughed and nodded their heads in agreement, and I immediately knew they had all experienced this challenge. If you are not in a relationship, the same challenges may arise with a best friend.

There are many stories about marital challenges arising from a retirement. I remember a story Roy McMurtry shared with me during his interview. “People sometimes say, ‘God, at 84, Roy, why the hell aren’t you retired?’” And he’d say, “Well, to some extent, because my wife reminds me from time to time that our wedding vows do not include lunch. And so, she’s still putting up with me, 59 years later.”

Garry, a retired teacher, told me the following story:

“The first day my wife retired, I came home from the fitness club at about 10 in the morning, and she had already done the laundry. She sat down with me and said, ‘Now what are we going to do?’ I reminded her that there was no “we” for over 30 years. We left the house every morning and we wouldn’t see each other until 4 or 5 o’clock in the afternoon. That seemed to have worked for 30 years, so why change it now?”

The media is filled with stories about the challenges of retirement and the stress it places on marriage. I completed 100 interviews and found that people did have marital challenges arising from a retirement, but if the relationships were strong, these new challenges were just like previous stresses. The couples dealt with them in the same resilient way they dealt with other ups and downs. They supported each other and moved through the stress successfully.

Lack of Socializing

Many of our friends are often work colleagues. When at work, we spent time with colleagues during coffee breaks, lunches, and after-work activities. If a lot of our socializing revolved around work, after we retire, we may experience a sudden decrease as this socializing abruptly ends. This is also true if many of our non-work friends are still working and not available to spend time with us during the day. This can be a difficult period resulting in isolation and depression if not dealt with proactively.

John, an investment manager, told me the following story:

“Most of my friendships were work related. My work life was very office oriented. Suddenly, when I retired, I had nowhere to go in the morning. Since my social life was at work and was very much a part of my day, there was a sudden drop off in my social life. I quickly found that all of my social networks at work disintegrated."

Transition Projects

As people enter Stage 2, the Transition Zone, they desire to fill their days with activity. Initially, some people go on a 'retirement' trip. Others turn to, 'Transition Projects'; activities that can quickly fill their time, require little preparation, and can be launched immediately. These projects include home and cottage renovations, organizing garages or basement storage 'junk' rooms, putting years of family photos into albums, etc. When Jane, a psychology professor, retired, she organized some home renovations they had been putting off due to a lack of time. She also organized her son's wedding, a task that would have been far more complicated had she been working at the time.

Elco, a former corporate CEO, described his transition in the following way:

"After retirement, my wife and I got on a plane and flew to Vancouver. We took a cruise to Alaska and then rented an SUV in Vancouver and drove to Calgary. We were gone four weeks. I did no planning prior to retirement. I struggled for about a year after retirement. I didn't want to do anything. It took about a year to get work out of my system. During that time, I did a lot of work on projects around the house. The first day back, I began sorting out family pictures, framing them, and hanging them. I spent months doing this. Then I sorted our CDs. It was a tough period, but I needed a break from my work routine."

These Transition Projects serve an important role: they give us immediate activities to busy ourselves while we decompress from the daily work routine. They also give us time to distance ourselves from 30 or more years of work routines. During this transitional period, we develop new routines and begin thinking about the future.

Personal Inventory

As we begin thinking about the future, it is helpful to complete a Personal Inventory. The Personal Inventory includes listing things, such as:

- Personal and technical skills;
- Things you liked doing at work and things you disliked doing;
- Hobbies you had when you were younger but gave up for busy work and family life during your middle years;
- Hobbies or interests you are currently involved in;
- New interests you have thought about but never had the time to pursue;
- Learning interests or new skills you would like to explore; and
- Issues or activities you are passionate about and would like to get involved in.

Your Personal Inventory will assist in determining how you'll spend your time in the third chapter of your life.

Reviewing your retirement finances is also an important part of your Personal Inventory. Do you need to earn additional income during the next phase of your life? Are you interested in work as a Protirement activity even if earning additional retirement income is not an issue?

Many Baby Boomers are concerned that they haven't saved sufficiently for their retirement. There are a few reasons for this. Some Boomers lost a significant part of their retirement savings during the 2008 market crash. Others thought they had saved enough, but with the reality that they may live another 20 or 30 years, they are concerned that they may not have enough to last that long, especially when their later years may be very costly. Also, some Boomers are unable to save sufficiently for retirement due to lower wages, lack of work-based pension plans, tuition fees, and other life expenses.

Some Boomers are fortunate and have excellent work-based pension plans that will provide them with sufficient retirement income. Others have been able to save sufficiently and build their own retirement funds. Nevertheless, many of these Boomers, who do not require additional retirement income, still decide to work after retirement for reasons other than money. They want to stay engaged in life, to have the challenge that comes with a job, for the social status, for their personal identity, and to socialize with colleagues.

The Personal Inventory helps people sort out the above issues and plan for Stage 3, Protirement.

Difficulty with the Transition Stage

We constantly hear stories of retirees who are floundering, haven't found new interests, are depressed, and sometimes experiencing marital discord. I found that these challenges usually occur because they are having difficulty in Stage 2, the Transition Zone. Transitioning from 'Retirement' to 'Protirement' can be a difficult process. When people are uncomfortable with change, cannot embrace new activities, are uncomfortable making new friends, and/or anxious about limited retirement funds, they are vulnerable to getting 'stuck' in the Transition Zone. They may be unable to recreate a new 'mission' or meaning in life. They may find it challenging to replace the role work filled in their life. When this occurs, and they are unable to move into the third Stage, Protirement, they may flounder in the Transition Zone. These are the people who say they wish they hadn't retired.

The positive part of this story is that all the individuals I spoke with eventually moved into the Protirement Stage. It took anywhere from weeks to years to make the transition into Protirement, but everyone eventually made the transition.

Stage 3: Protirement

Stage 3, Protirement, occurs as Boomers begin to engage in new activities. As mentioned in Chapter 1, the origin of the word "Protirement" came from combining parts of two words: **pro** active + re **tirement.** My definition of Protirement is:

"...the pursuit of fulfilling activities in the third chapter of our lives, after we retire. Some people choose to 'not retire', or to 'retire gradually' as their protirement activity."

Mystery writer, Louise Penny, in her book, *The Nature of the Beast*[4], wonderfully described Protirement:

Myrna laughed. "I know what you mean. When I quit my job as a psychologist, I felt guilty. This isn't our parent's generation, Armand. Now people have many chapters to their lives. When I stopped being a therapist I asked myself one question. What do I really want to do? Not for my friends, not for my family. Not for perfect strangers. But for me. Finally. It was my turn, my time. And this is yours, Armand. Yours and Reine-Marie's. What do you really want?"

As we enter the Protirement Stage, we have the opportunity to begin focusing on fulfilling and meaningful activities. During my interviews, people often talked about the joy they experienced when following their passions during their Protirement. As we do this, we begin re-developing aspects of our lives that were sometimes compromised during our work lives.

In Stage 3, Protirement, Boomers create new daily routines, develop a new sense of self, a new social status, a new identity, and often develop new friendships.

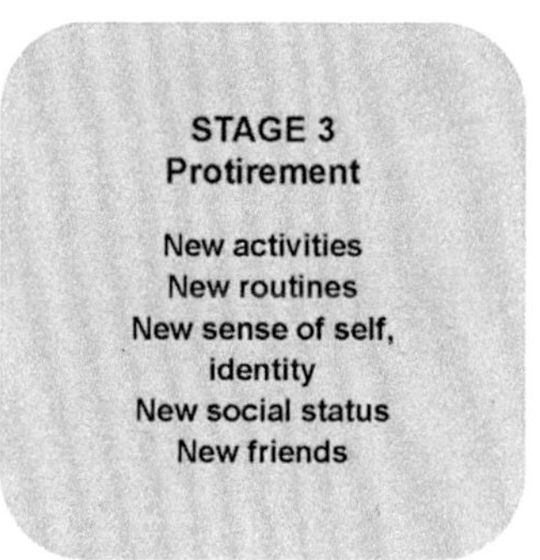

As we engage in new Protirement activities, new routines quickly evolve to replace old work routines.

Claire's transition was quick:

"I knew there were going to be a lot of things to do when I retired, because I was looking after my mother and spending time with my two grandsons. My mother was getting worse and worse so it took up more and more of my time."

Rosemary, a University Dean of Arts, became a volunteer at a hospice and described her new identity in the following way:

"I know that I loved being a leader, in charge and directing. But that is what I love *not* doing now. Now, I love being part of a team, and not the head of something. I love the fact that it doesn't all rest on me."

During the Protirement Stage, as you engage in new activities a new sense of self, a new identity, and a new social status begins to emerge. David, a retired social worker described this well:

"Your job is who you are, like it or not, and when you retire, you lose the status that comes with it. You should never underestimate the importance of your social needs and status needs. CESO (Canadian Executive Search Organization) filled those needs for me after I retired. I was so lucky finding CESO at that time." David became a volunteer with CESO and for the next 15 years, made 27 trips to developing countries as a volunteer advisor. He now works in the CESO office assisting in recruiting new 'Protired' volunteers.

For some people, retirement does not result in a loss of friends since their friends were not work related as Mario, a retired school administrator, explained:

"My social friends were not part of my educational work group so, when I retired, I still had those friends. I still get together with my educational work friends, as well."

For others, who have lost their friends, like John, a retired investment manager, whose friendship group was heavily connected to work, they have the opportunity of finding new friends as they get involved in new Protirement activities.

Moving Through the Stages

No retirement stage is exclusive. It is common to have one foot in Stage 1; dealing with career loss, while already beginning the transition into Stage 2; dealing with the lack of routines. Everyone journeys through the three stages at their own pace. Some people, like Mario, moved quickly through Stages 1 and 2. He had already decided, before announcing his retirement, that he was going to buy and operate a burger franchise. Others move through the stages slowly, like Gil Amelio, a retired CEO in the IT industry, who struggled for a few years in Stage 2 before moving onto an exciting new career as a transformation consultant in the IT industry. Rosemary, is another example of someone who straddled both Stages 1 and 2. She described the challenge of feeling sadness about the loss of her career (Stage 1) while also struggling with the loss her of identity as dean (Stage 2).

The diagram below highlights the overlap between Stages.

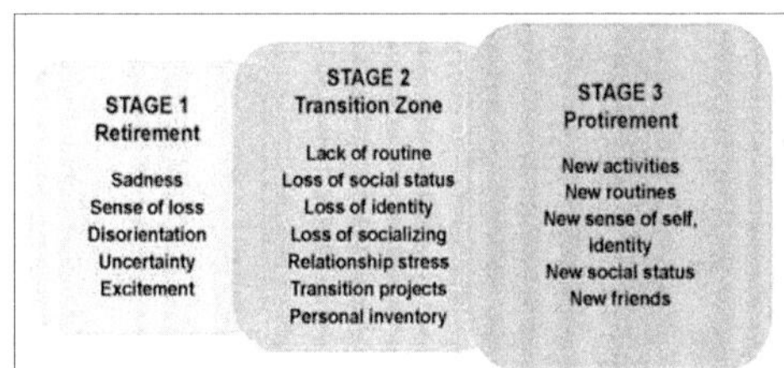

It is important to remember that everyone goes through these Stages at their own pace. No one's journey is the same. What is important, from the advice that people gave during their interviews, is that people strategically make decisions, and take action, during their career, to lessen the difficulty in transitioning through these Stages. We will discuss this advice in the next chapter.

The Second Curve

Charles Handy, an Irish author/philosopher specializing in organizational behavior and management, designed the Second Curve to describe the change process for individuals and organizations. When applying Handy's Second Curve[5] to the Protirement change process, the following occurs:

An individual usually retires when they are at the height of their career, or high on the Work curve, located near Stage 1 in the diagram below. At that point, as they decide to retire and enter Stage 2, the Transition Zone, they jump onto the "Second Curve" and begin the transition process toward a new journey.

The Second Curve

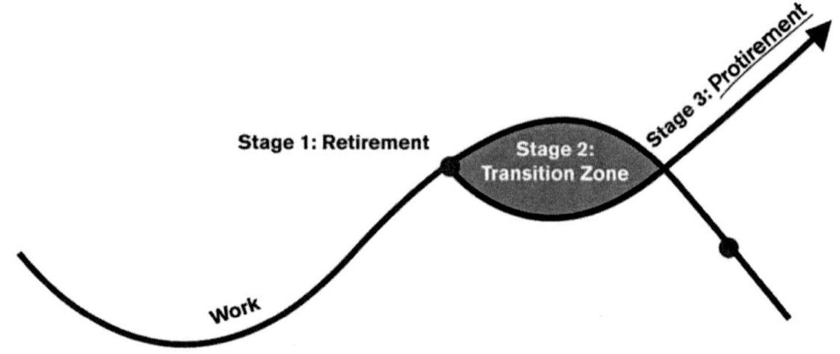

Charles Handy: The Second Curve

When you jump onto the Second Curve, you enter the Transition Zone and begin dealing with the change. At this point, your productivity usually decreases while you are adjusting to the change. Eventually, the curve bends upward along with your increased productivity. While you are in Stage 2, you can expect to experience challenges because of the unknowns in the Transition Zone. As you begin to resolve the transitional unknowns, you climb upward until you eventually move into Stage 3, Protirement. Protirement is where you begin to embrace new activities and a new fulfilling lifestyle.

The more prepared you are, as you move up the first Curve, i.e. your Work Curve, toward retirement and the beginning of Stage 1 (Retirement), the easier Stage 2 (the Transition Zone) will be. It is helpful to begin certain planning processes during your Work life, and prior to your decision to retire, to ease the transition onto the Second Curve. This does not mean that it is necessary to do so. We each have our own planning preferences, but it will facilitate the transition if some planning is done ahead of Stage 1.

Protirement Checkerboard

Through the analysis of the 100 interviews, I identified 17 Baby Boomer Protirement Categories. These are summarized in the following Protirement Checkerboard.

Not Retired/ Gradually Retiring	Contingency Workers	New Careers/Jobs	Seniorpreneurs
Caregivers	Political Activists	Hobbyists	Corporate Side Hustles
Travel Enthusiasts	Community Builders	Socializers	Writers/ Performers
Health Enthusiasts	Life Long Learners	Philanthropists	Family Enthusiasts

Life Enthusiasts

Research shows that many Baby Boomers aren't ready to completely retire from the work force, for financial as well as lifestyle reasons. This is evident on the Protirement Checkerboard where the first four of the 17 Protirement Categories are work related. The decision to continue working will be discussed in greater detail in Chapter 5. These four categories are further described below:

Not Retire or Gradually Retire – Some Boomers decide not to retire when they turn 65, but rather chose to stay in their current job full time, while others gradually decrease their workload over a number of years.

Contingency Work – These Boomers chose to retire and then accept project work or temporary shift work from their employer rather than a regular, ongoing schedule.

New Career or Job – These Boomers retire then start a new career or job, often in a totally new field.

"Seniorpreneur" – These Boomers start up their own businesses and become entrepreneurs. As discussed in Chapter 4, Boomers over 50 are the fastest growing age group embracing business start-ups throughout the developed world.

The remaining 12 Protirement Categories represent non-work relate activities. They are described as follows:

Caregivers – Many Boomers are involved as caregivers for parents, partners, children, grandchildren, and friends.

Political Activists – Some Boomers chose to become involved in politics as elected officials or as political volunteers at the municipal, regional, provincial, and/or federal levels.

Hobbyists – Many Boomers take up a hobby or spend more time in their favorite hobbies. There are 1000s of different hobbies, including: knitting, photography, reading, golfing, painting, renovations, music, dancing, scrap booking, horseback riding, archery, and many, many more.

Corporate Side Hussles – Some Boomers who worked in the corporate sector really enjoy that environment and want to continue in it after they retire. Protirement corporate side hustles include corporate directorships, Angel Investing, and business mentoring start-ups.

Travel Enthusiasts – Many Boomers like to travel but some make it a significant focus of their Protirement lifestyles. Travel enthusiasts travel locally, across North America, and internationally. Seventeen different travel venture types have emerged within the Boomer generation.

Community Builders – Many Boomers engage in a wide variety of volunteer work. Because these volunteers have an incredibly positive impact on their communities I have called them Community Builders. These Community Builders are volunteers on Boards of Directors and in direct service with community groups, health organizations, sports clubs, recreation programs, faith organizations, service clubs, advocacy groups, social service agencies, mental health programs, etc.

Socializers – These Boomers have sometimes been called social butterflies because they love to move from group to group and are known for bringing groups of people together. These Boomers organize regular meetings for varying purposes.

Writers/Performers – Some Boomers love to write and/or perform. Boomers are authors of non-fiction, fiction, poetry, blogs, music, magazine articles, and more. Some also enjoy performing music, poetry, plays, etc.

Health Enthusiasts – These Boomers take their health very seriously. They enjoy regular physical exercise, brain exercise, nutritional health, and mental wellness.

Life Long Learners – These Boomers appreciate and enjoy ongoing learning, in both formal & informal settings.

Philanthropists – Although many Boomers donate to charity, a small group spend some of their time developing formal funds or foundations to focus their giving on causes that are important to them.

Family Enthusiasts – These Boomers love to spend regular time with immediate and/or extended family, especially grandchildren.

Life Enthusiasts – These Boomers enjoy sampling the above activities without specializing in any one. They are like people who enjoy sampling all of the different foods on a buffet without having any one favorite.

In addition to embracing different Protirement activities, I found that many Baby Boomers are multi-taskers—does that surprise you? They are often engaged in a number of these Protirement activities at the same time. Many Boomers have one primary Protirement activity and spend lesser amounts of time on other secondary Protirement activities. Some Boomers divide their time among several activities.

The Protirement Checkerboard provides Boomers with a template to begin exploring their passions. The *Life 3.0 Workbook*, provides you with a template to begin exploring the categories on the checkerboard with the goal of developing your personalized Protirement Checkerboard.

The next chapter explores advice on how to make the transition from work to Protirement easier.

CHAPTER 3: PROTIREMENT ADVICE

"Protirement is a journey, not a destination!
Unknown

When I began the interviews, I had no idea that my final question—"What advice would you give your children or friends to make their transition from work to Protirement easier than it was for you?"—would result in a wealth of advice. I asked people to focus on lifestyle advice and *not* financial advice. As mentioned in the introduction, the second part of Protirement Planning, focuses on lifestyle.

I received over 400 bits of advice from my interviewees. As I analyzed their comments, I found that the advice fell into two categories. The first category is Pre-Retirement Advice and deals with advice related to your lifestyle while you are still working. The second category is Protirement Advice and deals with lifestyle advice for people who are on the verge of retiring or who have already retired and transitioned in to Stage 2 or Stage 3. This chapter will address both categories.

Pre-Retirement Advice

When giving advice, many people talked about: a) wishing they had done certain things before they retired in preparation for life after work, or b) what they had done to prepare for life after work.

Their advice regarding 'Pre-Retirement' planning covered the following four themes:

- Have non-work interests before you retire;
- Plan before you retire;
- Health – Keep Active; and
- Don't retire too early.

Each theme is highlighted below.

1. Have non-work interests before you retire

Of all the advice given, "Have non-work interests" was mentioned the most.

Having interests outside of work ensures that we have some activities to engage in when we first retire, especially during the Transition Stage. Being involved in these non-work activities prior to retirement will allow us to maintain our involvement in familiar activities and with some non-work colleagues as we enter Stage 2.

Part of our personal identity and social status is often connected to these non-work activities, which can provide an important bridge between our work-life identity and Protirement. My involvement in Rotary, while I was working, is an example of how my non-work activity and my identity as a Rotarian carried over after I retired, and assisted me as I entered the Transition Zone.

These non-work activities also help us develop friendships outside of our work environment so we aren't isolated once our work-life ends. These non-work activities can fill in some of the gaps in our routine as we transition toward Protirement.

2. Plan before you retire

"Plan before your retire" was the second most frequently mentioned advice theme. Advice included comments like:

- "Develop a personal learning plan";
- "Define what 'turns you on' and look for ways to use your skills in retirement";
- "What gives you most satisfaction in your daily life? Continue to do that in your retirement";

- "Ask yourself, 'What's the most useful thing to do? What's the most interesting thing to do? Then do it.'"; and
- "Look at your career from a 30,000-foot view and pluck out the things you love most."

Although most of us have spent time developing a Financial Retirement Plan, we have not spent the same amount of time developing a Lifestyle Plan. The two plans complete the Protirement Planning circle and should support each other.

Protirement Plan

The *Life 3.0 Workbook* uses the advice outlined in this book to assist you in developing your own personalized Protirement Lifestyle Plan. Once you have developed your Lifestyle Plan, review it with your Financial Advisor to ensure that both plans are compatible and support one another.

Whether you are five years away from Stage 1, on the verge of Stage 1, or already retired and in Stage 2, the Transition Zone or even Stage 3, Protirement Lifestyle Planning is a useful exercise. It ensures that you have accounted for all of the different aspects related to the three stages of the Protirement Process.

3. Health - Keep Active

"Health - Keep Active" was also a frequent advice theme. People talked about the importance of keeping physically active during their working years and how, being in good physical condition, made it easier for them when they retired. People expressed this advice in many different ways, including comments such as:

- "Pay attention to your health";
- "Take care of your health";
- "No matter what your career, maintain a wellness program that is suited to you";
- "Keep yourself healthy, watch your diet";
- "Exercise";
- "Enjoy sports"; and
- "Keep physically fit".

4. Don't retire too quickly

Many people warned against retiring too quickly. They talked about not retiring if you love your work, retiring gradually, and not retiring if finances are a concern. Comments such as the following, reflect this advice.

- "If you're happy in your work, keep at it";
- "Don't be in a hurry to retire if you are still productive and enjoying your work";
- "If you enjoy your job, stay with it";
- "If you can wind down slowly, it is better to gradually retire";
- "Keep busy, step away gradually";
- "Work part-time if you like what you are doing"; and
- "Consider your finances, and if you can save up more money gradually, do so."

Protirement Advice

There were eight types of advice related to your Protirement lifestyle. Topics included:

- Keep Active;
- Follow your passion;
- Give back to your community;
- Maintain relationships in the community;
- Try new things, continuous learning;
- Maintain family relationships;
- Retirement doesn't mean quitting from life; and
- Keep a positive attitude.

1. Keep Active

"Keep Active" advice covered two themes, including general advice about physical activity and more specifically, Brain Health. Over 30% of the people interviewed shared stories about people dying within two years of retirement. The common perception was that they died because of inactivity and a lack of involvement in post-retirement activities. Although the research is mixed on whether this outcome can really be proven, anecdotally, people are convinced it is true and are making lifestyle decisions based on these perceptions.

We know inactivity affects our physical health and obesity rates. We also know that lack of engagement in activities can lead to social isolation and, potentially, depression, which can then lead to deteriorating physical health. Whether or not there is a definitive link to early death due to inactivity after retirement, we do know that inactivity and lack of engagement impact health negatively. Therefore, we can assume the following advice will positively impact your Protirement.

a) Physical Activity

There were many comments about staying active in your Protirement including:

- "Stay active";
- "It is better to wear out than rust out";
- "Always exercise";
- "Get involved in sports";

b) Brain Health

There were numerous comments about the importance of brain health. People shared stories of how they choose to do things like Sudoku and crosswords, playing bridge, reading, and working to keep their brains active. With the rise in dementia and Alzheimer's, Boomers are looking for new ways to keep their brains healthy. Their advice is as follows:

- "Keep your brain working";
- "The brain is like a muscle, it needs exercise";
- "Stay mentally active";

- "Keep reading and stretching your brain"; and
- "Keep your mind active."

2. Follow your Passion

Many of those interviewed mentioned, "Following your passion" and "Having a Purpose" during the third chapter of your life. I have divided this advice into these two categories:

a) Follow your Passion

There was a strong sentiment that Protirement was a time to embrace the activities you are passionate about. We should pursue activities we are passionate about but may not have had time to do when we were working. Comments included:

- "Do things that you are passionate about";
- "Have some interests of the heart and interests of the mind to keep yourself involved";
- "Figure out what gives you pleasure in life and find ways to do it"; and
- "Find your passion."

b) Have a Purpose

Linked to being passionate about our Protirement activities were comments addressing the importance of "Having a Purpose" in our Protirement. The Boomers of the 60s who wanted to change the world are now talking about having a purpose during the third chapter of their lives. They said things, like:

- "You have to have a purpose in life";
- "Examine your values, they will help you decide what you are going to do in your Protirement"; and
- "Find a new identity, a new purpose in life."

3. Give Back to your Community

There were many comments about giving back to the community through volunteering. People said things like:

- "We have had a wonderful ride, it is time to give back";
- "Pursue volunteerism, give back"; and

- "Be involved in the community; find projects that build on your strengths."

4. Maintain Relationships in the Community

Advice related to maintaining relationships and socializing include:

- "Friendship is very important, visit with people every day";
- "Look after your social interactions, avoid isolation"; and
- "You have to do something that involves people."

5. Try New Things: Continuous Learning

Boomers see their Protirement years as a time to explore, learn new activities, and continue growing. Advice included:

- "Don't be afraid to try new things";
- "Be open to continual learning"; and
- "Always be a student."

6. Maintain Relationships

Boomers were keenly aware of the importance of family in their Protirement years. I have divided the advice into the following two sub-categories:

a) Maintain Partner Relationships

Boomers know it's important to maintain healthy relationships with partners during the transition to Protirement. Advice included comments, such as:

- "Be aware of the adjustment involved in suddenly spending 24/7 with your partner after you retire"; and
- "Be sensitive to changes in your lifestyle that impact your relationship with your spouse."

b) Maintain Family Relationships

Interviewees also spoke on the importance of maintaining family relationships. Their advice included:

"Stay engaged with your family, whatever that means for each family";

- "Strong family ties can really enhance your retirement"; and
- "Value family more as you go along."

7. Retirement Doesn't Mean Quitting Life

Boomers are conscious of being far more active in the third chapter of their lives than previous generations. Boomers are cautious about the old retirement paradigm not being imposed upon them and want to make sure that active life continues after Stage 1, Retirement. Their advice included comments, such as:

- "Retirement doesn't mean quitting from life";
- "You really should not retire from life";
- "Studies are quite clear, if you retire, stay at home, and drink beer all day, you will die early"; and
- "'Retire' isn't in my vocabulary. I believe you don't retire until you die."

8. Keep a Positive

Boomers are very mindful of the importance of maintaining a positive outlook on life. The final area of advice related to the importance of "keeping a positive attitude." Types of advice included:

- "Watch your attitude, stay positive";
- "It's so easy to be critical and get negative";
- "Don't sweat the small stuff"; and
- "If you wake up in the morning and you're of good health and good mind, then figure out a way to enjoy the balance of the day."

The advice given by people interviewed for Life 3.0, provides a clear road map for Boomers who plan prior to retiring, as well as for those already retired, in transition, or already enjoying their Protirement.

We can truly enhance our Protirement years by following the simple advice of those who have already made the journey before us. Their experiences and thoughts on making the Protirement journey an enjoyable and fulfilling one is filled with rich, simple advice. I truly appreciate everyone's willingness to offer their honest insight.

CHAPTER 4: BRIDGE EMPLOYMENT: WORKING BEYOND RETIREMENT

"The happiest people I know are the ones that are still working. The saddest are the ones who are retired. Six years ago, Sinatra announced his retirement. He's still working."
George Burns

Introduction

Some Boomers are choosing not to retire when they turn 65, while others are choosing to retire but then return to the workforce. My research identified four different categories of work-related Protirement activities, referred to as Bridge Employment. Before exploring these activities, let's have a quick look at what the research says about work after retirement.

What does the research say?

Why are Boomers working beyond 65? Much has been written about this new phenomenon.

Let's first explore the statistics. In 2012, in both Canada and the United States, almost 32% of 65 to 69 year olds were still working full-time or part-time[6].

A 2014 poll by the American Association of Retired People (AARP)[7] reported that 70% of Boomers planned to delay their retirement beyond the age of 65. In a 2012 CIBC poll, 57% of

Canadian Boomers stated that they planned on working beyond the age of 65, while in a 2011 Bank of Nova Scotia poll, 70% of Canadian respondents reported that they planned on working beyond the age of 65.[8]

A 2014 report by the Conference Board of Canada noted that while 60% of current retirees thought their retirement incomes were sufficient, 51% of those aged 44 to 60 and 60% of those aged 65+ said they will continue working after they retire. [9]

Although the percentages vary in these polls, the main theme is consistent: a majority of Baby Boomers are planning on working after they turn 65. There are a number of reasons for this, including:

- Many Boomers lost part of their retirement savings during the 2008 economic downturn;
- Others weren't able to accrue sufficient retirement savings due to lower incomes and/or other financial pressures during their working years;
- Many Boomers do not have employer supported pension plans;
- Some Boomers want to continue to work to supplement their retirement savings to do 'fun' things their savings plans may not cover;
- Many early retirement plans did not take into account the reality that Boomers may live 20 or 30 years beyond their retirement, creating concerns about outliving their savings; and
- To complicate things, if Boomers live another 20 or 30 years, and if their health begins to deteriorate, they are concerned they may not have sufficient retirement savings to cover the high costs of home support, retirement homes, and/or nursing home facilities.

There are also reasons other than finances that underlay Baby Boomers desire to work into the third chapter of their lives, including the reality that work provides:

- A purpose;
- A sense of identity;
- An increase in self-worth;
- A routine and structure to daily life;

- Intellectual stimulation; and
- Social interaction.

Why have Boomers' attitudes changed toward working after 65?

Boomers' attitudes about working after 65 have changed, and here are the four reasons why.

Health

Baby Boomers are healthier and will live longer than any previous generation. In 1921, Canadians lived to an average age of 57. Fast forward to 2011, and the average age increased to 81.7, an increase of almost 25 years. Baby Boomers have embraced healthy lifestyles, including: healthier diets, increased physical exercise, a cessation in smoking, wearing seat belts, etc. These have had a significant positive impact on health and life span. Also, during the past 30 years, there have been exponential advancements in health care, leading to fewer deaths from illnesses like heart disease and cancer.

The age of the onset of age-related disabilities has also risen. According to Statistics Canada, debilitating disabilities affect Canadians, on average, around the age of 77. That means Baby Boomers have at least 12 years of active, productive life after the traditional retirement age of 65. Many Boomers will live well into their 80s before any serious disabilities affect their daily activities.

New Paradigm of Aging

Sociologists speak of life in three stages: Childhood (Birth to 21); Adulthood (21 – 65); and Old Age (65 – 75). As discussed in Chapter 1, I referred to this as the Old Paradigm. Retirement occurred during the Old Age phase:

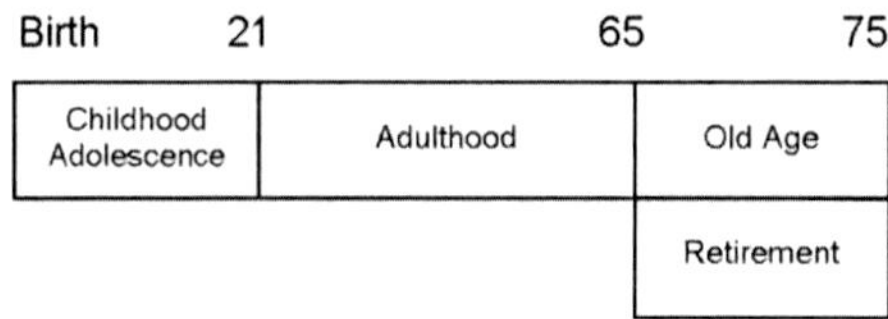

Baby Boomers with increased health and extended lifespan have changed this dialogue. It is clear that a healthy period beyond adulthood occurs before old age sets in and seriously impacts an individual's capacity to actively enjoy life. The three stages in the New Paradigm include Childhood/Adolescence (Birth to 25); Adulthood (25 to 80); and Older Adults (80 to 100). The active period, after retirement (varies from whenever one retires through Older Adulthood) is the Protirement stage.

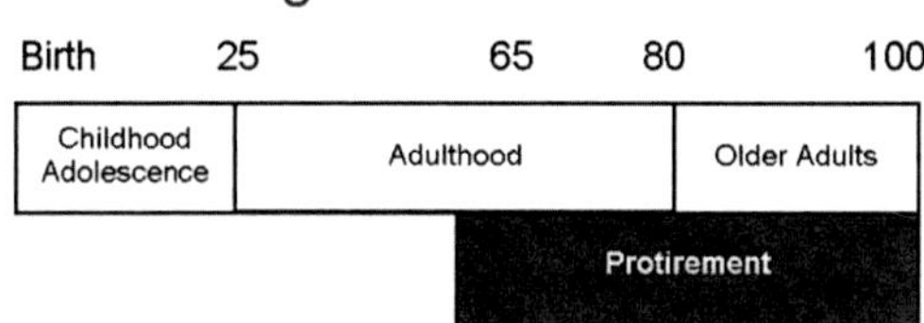

According to a Pew Research Center poll, Boomers don't consider themselves old until around 72 years of age.[10] There is a more informal definition of "old age" among Boomers - when someone is 10 years older than they are. Therefore, Boomers may never feel old, as long as they know people at least 10 years older than themselves.

Attitudes

Boomers tend to be hard working and ambitious. They grew up being known as the "me" generation, wanting to be engaged in satisfying and self-validating work. Turning 65 doesn't just change these attitudes. Boomers see no reason to suddenly become disengaged from work. Their self-identity and social status are intertwined with their work. Giving up their work identity often results in a feeling of irrelevancy and redundancy, feelings that often drive Baby Boomers back into work settings.

Finances

Many Boomers' retirement savings significantly decreased during the 2008 financial crisis. A 2012 CIBC poll found that 45% of Canadians in their 50s had saved less than $100,000 for their retirement, while 53% said they planned on working part-time or full-time after they retired.[11] An AARP report said that 75% of Americans between 55 and 64 had less than $30,000 in retirement savings, while a Merrill Lynch study found that 62% of US Boomers planned on working after they retired.[13]

Caregiving

As the "sandwich" generation, Boomers often find themselves caring for both their children and elderly parents. Having started families later in life, some Boomers are still supporting children who are in college or just starting out in their careers. At the same time, Boomers often have elderly parents to care for. As Boomers age, caring for a partner or close friend often becomes a consideration, as well.

Some Boomers are also caring for grandchildren. As their children start careers and families, child care and housing expenses become a strain on their income. They are, therefore, frequently turning to retired parents for help with child care.

Bridge Employment: Work-Related Protirement Categories

'Encore Jobs'; 'Encore Careers'; 'Redirection', and 'Serial Retirement' are terms used to describe the phenomenon of Boomers returning to the work force after retirement.

Statistics Canada calls these types of post-retirement activities, Bridge Employment.[14] Using the information I collected through 100 interviews, I have identified four categories of post retirement Bridge Employment. These include:

Not Retired/ Gradually Retiring	Contingency Workers	New Careers/Jobs	Seniorpreneurs

Work-Related Protirement Stories

Throughout the interviews, many people commented on how important work was to them beyond the age of 65. Here is a sampling of their comments:

Heather C. (Now 75), executive search consultant, Protirement Activity – **Not Retired**/Gradually Retiring: "I would have been eligible for retirement at 65 but I didn't want to retire because I loved what I did. I came here (a new employer) and now I am 75. I still love what I do."

Kwame K. (Now 73), family physician, Protirement Activity – Not Retired/**Gradually Retiring**: "I now work four days a week and take Wednesdays off for myself. A few years ago, I joined a friend and we built a hospital in Ghana; the Ghana Canada Hospital. I go to Ghana twice a year and work in the hospital."

Kevin F. (Retired 65, Now 72), family physician, Protirement Activity – **Contingency Worker:** "I have done locums in about 10 different offices since I retired. They were both short and long term locums, when other doctors needed a replacement. I am now going to stop doing locums."

John M. (Retired 58, Now 65), former municipal CAO, Protirement Activity – **New Career**: "With a second career, I had no intention of going to work every day. I go to Burlington two days a week, where there are five staff in the office (John is Executive Director for a national church organization). I work from home most of the time. I have lots of phone meetings. I still play hockey twice a week, in the morning. I am able to set my schedule around things that I like to do."

John Dan J. (Retired 65, Now 83), former coal miner, Protirement Activity – **Seniorpreneur**: His daughter shares: "My dad still works in the restaurant. That keeps him young, keeps him going. He comes in early. He was here when we got here at 7:30 this morning. He already had the turkey in the oven, and he had just made the fish chowder. He also makes the coconut cream pies."

Each of the next four chapters will describe one of these four work-related Protirement Activities. The chapters begin with background research and then share personal Protirement Stories.

CHAPTER 5: PROTIREMENT CATEGORY #1: NOT RETIRED / GRADUALLY RETIRING

"I have chosen not to retire because I think there is lots I can share, lots of people that I can still help."
Betty-Lou S.

Introduction

Some people chose "Not to Retire or Gradually Retire." They love their jobs so much that they see no reason to retire. Not retiring is a growing trend among Baby Boomers. Heather, a 75-year-old executive search consultant told me, "I don't want to retire because I love what I do; it's part of my DNA."

As discussed in Chapter 3, some people are choosing to "not retire" for financial reasons, while others are choosing to "not retire" because they love their job, feel too young to retire, like the challenge of the job, and enjoy being engaged in work.

Facts about "Not Retired / Gradually Retire"

A majority of Baby Boomers are planning on working after they turn 65, and some of them are staying in their job but planning on retiring gradually by reducing their workload over a number of years. Employers are beginning to support this strategy so they do not lose a large portion of their Boomer employees at one time.

I've compiled the following stories to help illuminate what it means to gradually retire.

"Not Retired or Gradually Retiring" Protirement Stories

I interviewed 16 people who have chosen not to retire. They ranged in age from 65 to 84. They all loved their work and couldn't see life without it. Some had slowed down and were able to add other activities to their lives, while others were still working full-time.

Jim, a 74-year-old lawyer, is an example of someone who still works full-time but has delegated work to others in his firm. He also travels extensively with his wife while working remotely, using today's networking capabilities. Here's how he described his gradual transition:

"I slowed down a little bit on the work that I was doing and transferred it to others in the firm. As a lawyer, I always preached retirement planning for your business. So, my planning was and is a slow succession, continuing to do what I do well, and the things that I am not as fond of are passed on to others. This allows me greater time for the community, for my family, and being able to travel. One of the great things with the new electronic world is the ability to travel and to do business while you are away and to support staff while you are away."

Six of the people who had not retired were owners, partners, or principals in small businesses. The businesses dealt with human resources, financial management, cosmetology, executive search, legal matters, and real estate.

Anne, a 68-year-old owner of a human resources business, details her decision to continue working after 65:

"I'm working because I have to; but if I didn't have to, I'd still be working. I think if people want to retire early, they have to create a life for themselves outside of their business, and not a lot of entrepreneurs do that. And so, then they struggle, with: "what are they going to do after?"

One person interviewed was involved in federal politics. MP Rob Nicholson is a former cabinet minister, and is currently the Conservative Justice Critic. Rob was 65-years-old when interviewed and will be 67 when the next election is held. At this point, he still plans on running again in the next election.

When thinking about retirement, Rob described his future in politics by saying:

"I have had a great work life and enjoyed my career wherever I found myself. I will be 67 at the end of this term of government. I am not ready for retirement at this time and currently plan to run again in the next federal election, but will make a final decision when we are closer to that date."

I interviewed two well know musicians, Ronnie Hawkins, who was 81, and Liona Boyd, who was 67. Both are still active in their careers, although, Ronnie is slowing down due to health challenges. Liona Boyd still performs, and describes her choice to continue working:

"I have been lucky that my work, really, is my hobby; is my passion, my love. It never really seemed like work. Years later, I got musician's focal dystonia by multitasking. I had to quit for six years, so I guess I did retire, for six years. It was heartbreaking for me. I had a taste of early retirement and it was miserable. I had a taste of what it's like to be unable to play guitar; and now I'm very grateful: every time I step on the stage. I think how lucky I am."

I'll probably always be writing; I have a new album, it's coming out in 2017. It's called *No Remedy for Love*, from a quote by David Henry Thoreau: "There's no remedy for love but to love more," which is quite profound. I dedicated that song to Leonard Cohen."

Sometimes I do feel lonely these days because I sense my mortality. Prince Philip said to me, 'Once you start sensing your mortality, then you have to make some changes in your life.'"

Three individuals were working in the not-for-profit sector. Dan, 68 years old, is president of a large college, and Betty-Lou, 73 years old, is CEO of a community agency. Dr. George Wood, 75 years old, is general superintendent of the General Council of the Assemblies of God in the USA, and Chairman the World Assemblies of God Fellowship.

Betty-Lou talked about her decision not to retire:

"I have chosen not to retire because I still think there is lots that I can share; lots of people that I can help. I love being with people, I love having stimulating conversations and getting into debates with people. You have to keep your mind sharp. What keeps my brain active is trying to problem solve for my clients, and trying to keep this organization going down the right path."

Kwame was a 73-year-old pediatrician. Ken Goldman, 67 years old, was CFO of Yahoo.

Kwame described his decision not to retire at 65:

"A key to work for me is you have to love your job. If you don't love your job, you shouldn't be doing it. I love coming to work, I love doing what I do, my brain is still working, I am still good at it. So, at the age of 65, retirement wasn't on the table at all."

All 16 individuals spoke of continuing to work because they loved their jobs, one also spoke about financial reasons for continuing to work. Eight individuals were also involved in other Protirement activities such as hobbyists, travel enthusiasts, community builders, health enthusiasts, and philanthropists in addition to their work.

"Not Retired/Gradually Retiring" personal Protirement Stories follow.

Name:	Anne C.
Occupation:	Business Owner; Human Resources
Retirement Age:	55 until 57
Current Age:	68
Protirement Activities:	**Not Retired/Gradually Retiring**

My Protirement Story

I'm working because I have to; but if I didn't have to, I'd still be working. I think if people want to retire early, they have to create a life for themselves outside of their business, and not a lot of entrepreneurs do that. And so, then they struggle, with: "what are they going to do after?" You know, my brother said to me—my brother's been retired forever— "There's only so many games of golf you can play." I have a friend who worked for the police. He retired about ten years ago and they were spending every winter in Panama. He came to me last year and said, "I want a job." I said, "Jim, you've been out of the market for ten years, I don't know what I'm going to do with you." And he said to me, "Well, I'm fed up golfing; I'm fed up with Panama, I'm fed up."

So, early retirement may sound like a great deal, but make sure you've got something to do. For me, I don't know what I'd do. I would still work. Even if I could afford not to, I would still work. Because I just don't have anything else that gives me the same satisfaction and energy that work does. I could see myself getting in trouble if I didn't have work, because, outside of driving my family crazy, I don't know what I would do with myself all day.

My Advice

- Make sure you have something else to do when you retire.
- Create a life outside of your work while you are working so you have something to do when you retire.
- Or, if you love what you do, then keep right on doing it!

Name: Betty-Lou S.
Occupation: Non-Profit Executive
Retirement Age: Not Retired
Current Age: **73**
Protirement Activities: **Not Retired/Gradually Retiring;** Community Builder

My Protirement Story

I have chosen not to retire because I still think there is lots that I can share; lots of people that I can help. I love being with people, I love having stimulating conversations and getting into debates with people. You have to keep your mind sharp. My parents were great academics. My dad was an engineer who built bridges and dams, and my mom was a superintendent at the District School Board of Greater Montreal. They both wound up with dementia. I always remember the psychologist in Montreal telling us: “Let it be a lesson to keep our mind alert and active.” At that time, people were forced to retire and didn’t have an opportunity to keep their minds stimulated. What keeps my brain active is trying to problem solve for my clients and trying to keep this organization going down the right path.

When I do retire, I would like to mentor young people. Also, I have travelled a fair bit but haven’t been to Greece, it might be nice to do one more trip.

My husband has always allowed me to do what I have to do and to get to where I have to go. He has supported me intensely, with the understanding that this is my shtick not his. He has often said: “I have had my shtick and I have no need to be involved with yours.”

My Advice

- Keep your mind active.
- Discipline yourself to get up in the morning and have a purpose in your life.
- Do activities that keep your mind alert.
- Stay engaged in life.

Name:	Bill H.
Occupation:	Fund Development Consultant
Retirement Age:	Not Retired
Current Age:	72
Protirement Activities:	**Not Retired/Gradually Retiring;** Health Enthusiast; Family Enthusiast

My Protirement Story

When I got to 64, my brothers kept needling me about when I was going to retire. I said, "Never going to retire; I don't believe in it." They said, "Why?" I named a few friends who had retired and were dead two years later. I think retirement's a death sentence.

I'm worried that if I retire, I'll become a vegetable, or watch sports on TV and won't be that active. That's scary to me.

My wife's and my siblings and relatives are in Niagara. Since we're both from there we sold our Oakville house and bought a townhouse in Niagara (Welland).

When a client heard that I was coming back to Niagara they said, "Oh great! You can work for us more!" So, I'll probably keep my hand in with them, if they want me. I have another, similar, contract in Alliston; it's only a couple times a month. Both are great clients.

The townhouse we bought is surrounded by golf clubs, so, I said, "Next year, I plan on golfing three days a week." I'm planning on staying active. I'm a lifetime member of the Y and there's a fitness club in the townhouse complex. There are also a few of charities that I would enjoy working with.

My whole goal is to become more physically active. I haven't told my wife this, but I might even be able to help out with a high school football team. The guys I hung around with in high school are saying, "Bill, join our men's golf league next year." I'm looking for that kind of stuff.

I'm thinking of writing a book, but who needs another fundraising book? I'm toying with a few ideas. What I'll be able to do, I said to my wife, is take all the pictures we have, in boxes and on the computer, and I'm going to assemble them into some kind of a family history.

The other day my wife said, "Bill, starting in January, you do 50% of the housework." She has a lot of friends in Niagara and back in Oakville and so do I, and we both golf; so I have a feeling that we'll both be pretty busy.

My brothers and I are really close and they live in St. Catharines, so we will be able to see each other more regularly, especially golfing together a lot more.

My Advice

- Stay active.
- Do volunteer work.
- Continue to work full or part-time if you love what you are doing.

Name:	Dan Patterson
Occupation:	President, Niagara College
Retirement Age:	Not Retired
Current Age:	68
Protirement Activities:	**Not Retired/Gradually Retiring**

My Protirement Story

I think ageism is an issue. When people start approaching retirement age, it's often difficult to discuss the issue of retirement with friends and colleagues, when you are not quite sure. It's always a push-pull for me. I love the college and love my work. I'm also cognisant of the importance of knowing when to let go. The key is to surround yourself with people that can help guide you and arrive at the right time to make the decision.

I don't dislike the word *retirement*, but it's had baggage from previous generations. If you're in your 60s, you've grown up with a concept of retirement meaning slowing down and not being very productive any longer.

We have a retirees' association at the college and when I see them, I am always impressed on how happy they are and how great they look. So many have forged a very satisfying retirement life style and often they say they don't know how they had found the time to work! Clearly though, there are a number of people who have said, "Oh, I'm back now working, because I found it hard, my mind was not stimulated enough."

I encourage people to develop a personal learning plan, to write down two or three things that are important to them, and what kind of action they are going to take to achieve their plan. My learning plan is about "life after Niagara College." What would that look like in terms of hobbies, of consulting, international travel, or…?

I also talk about value-based leadership, or looking at the values that drive you. I think this helps you decide what kind of lifestyle you want for the future. At the end of the day, with retirement, I believe you're going to be much happier on the lane you choose, in life or in retirement, if you're driven by a set of values.

My Advice

- Develop a Personal Learning Plan, write down two or three things that are important to you for your retirement planning, and actions you are going to take to achieve those things.
- Examine your values, they will help you decide what you are going to do in your Protirement.

Name:	Dave K.
Occupation:	Consultant
Retirement Age:	66
Current Age:	72
Protirement Activities:	**Gradually Retiring;** Hobbyist; Writer/Performer

My Protirement Story

In 2010, I decided that consulting with international not-for-profit organizations had been wonderful, but I was really getting tired of travelling. I was weary of being away from home so much. My oldest friend died of cancer in 2010. I was also diagnosed with cancer that year. It brought home to me that you don't live forever. I was 66 at the time.

I found that there was work available here in Canada, and ended up doing some work closer to home. But it is nice to be working less and less, as time goes on. I always seem to have two or three interesting projects on the go that keep my mind going.

My wife, Holly and I had a desire to have a life together again, after my many years of travelling. Music has always been important to me. Although I have played the guitar for many years, and always took it with me, I couldn't take lessons or play with others while I was travelling. Once I stopped travelling I found a good music teacher and joined a jazz band. Holly is also in the band.

I enjoy downhill skiing. I used to teach downhill but hadn't skied in 40 years. I have taken up skiing again, and enjoy my music and reading. Spending time with my Holly is much more of a focus at this point in my life. We built our current home in 2002, on this country lot. We designed it to be low maintenance. Living in the country is very important to both of us.

My Advice

- Staying physically fit is important, especially as we age.
- Find a spiritual path of some sort.
- Find something that really engages your mind.
- Find someone to share it with.

Name:	Don R.
Occupation:	Entrepreneur; Owner of a Financial Management Firm
Retirement Age:	Not Retired
Current Age:	70
Protirement Activities:	**Not Retired/Gradually Retiring; Travel Enthusiast**; Community Builder; Health Enthusiast

My Protirement

Since 1994, when I launched Donro Financial, I have never worked more than nine months out of the year. The other months have always been taken up with travel and other activities. I played tennis all my life, golfed, and skied out west every year for a couple of weeks. I like chess and am an avid reader. I still run. I started competing in 5k to half marathon runs when I was in my 50s. I don't compete anymore.

I have a cottage in Nova Scotia and use for part of my three months off for relaxing, coming to grips with issues, and getting out of the mainstream. I do not have internet at the house. I have to drive down to the Annapolis Valley to use my cell phone. It breaks the habit and gives me a chance to unwind and distress.

I have also been in Rotary since 1980. I chartered the Lakeshore Club as its first president.

My Advice

- Maintain everything you enjoy doing, if possible.
- Don't slow down just because your friends do. As long as you can keep it up, keep it up.
- Watch your attitude, stay positive, it's so easy to be critical and get negative.

Name:	Dr. George Wood
Occupation:	General Superintendent of the General of the Assemblies of God in the USA and Chairman the World Assemblies of God Fellowship
Retirement Age:	Not Retired
Current Age:	75
Protirement Activities:	**Not Retired/Gradually Retiring**

My Protirement Story

I'm 75. Interestingly, all my life I planned to retire at 65. At the end of my 65th year, at our convention, I was elected as General Superintendent. I thought, "Well, okay; you know, this sounds like a great thing to do, and I would enjoy it." I had some ideas about what to do. I've continued to be re-elected and am up for election again in August. I'll probably let my name go up because I feel good. I run at a pace faster than my own kids. As long as I am mentally and physically able, and feel good about what I'm doing, I'll continue. I enjoy doing what I'm doing.

My daughter's son started at USC in January. Her husband is a little bit older than her, maybe seven years or so. They will probably be facing retirement in a few more years. They like to kick back, and just travel and do things. My son is the Executive Editor for our publications. They have an eight-year-old. They also have two little girls they adopted after fostering them the last three years. They are four and three years old. He's 48.We were talking this morning; when he is 65, they'll be about 18 and 20. I don't know if he'll want to retire then or not, so it'll be interesting.

I hear stories, I don't have any empirical data for this, that people who retire and do nothing, die fairly soon. I don't know if that's true or not.

My Advice

- Do what you enjoy doing.
- Make it meaningful, don't just live for self.
- Volunteer or invest in other people's lives.

Name: Heather C.
Occupation: Partner in Executive Search Firm
Retirement Age: Not Retired
Current Age: 76
Protirement Activities: **Not Retired/Gradually Retiring;** Hobbyist; Community Builder; Health Enthusiast; Family Enthusiast

My Protirement Story

I would have been eligible for retirement at 65 but I didn't want to retire because I loved what I did. I came here and now I am 76. I still love what I do. I do a lot of public leadership search.

I have always been very active. I go to the gym early every morning and work out for an hour. I still play the piano and enjoy writing. The opportunity to help not-for-profits at a governance level is also important, and as long as I feel I am adding value to those causes, I will continue my volunteer efforts as a Board member.

I do think that 75 is the new 65. In many ways, people have to know themselves and what drives them. The fact that my mother was a single working mother had an influence on me. When other kids were travelling in high school I was working, so I got a lot of joy out of that. I worked for the government of Nova Scotia Department of Highways, taught music to kids, and played, coached and refereed basketball. I was always working, it's part of my DNA, and I think everyone has to know their DNA. I have friends who are retired, painting, travelling a lot, and doing many different things.

My Advice

- Think carefully about your family situation. Think about the family dynamic, do you want to travel? What are your interests outside of work? What would you do together or separately?
- Stay engaged with your family, whatever that means for each family.
- Your health is a consideration, exercise is important to staying healthy.
- What gives you the most satisfaction in your daily lives? Continue that in your retirement.

Name:	Jim S.
Occupation:	Lawyer
Retirement Age:	Not Retired
Current Age:	74
Protirement Activities:	**Not Retired/Gradually Retiring;** Travel Enthusiast; Community Builder; Family Enthusiast

My Protirement Story

I thought about, I guess that it just sort of happened. I slowed down a little bit on the work that I was doing and transferred it to others in the firm. As a lawyer, I always preached retirement planning for your business. So my planning was and is a slow succession, continuing to do what I do well and the things that I am not as fond of are passed on to others. This allows me greater time for the community, for my family, and being able to travel. One of the great things with the new electronic world is the ability to travel and to do business and support staff while you are away.

I have always been involved in the community, including United Way, Big Brothers, Big Sisters, and Chamber of Commerce. Currently my main two community commitments are Rotary and Pathstone Mental Health. Until recently, I was also involved in the planning of the 2019 British Open at the Royal Portrush Golf Club in Northern Ireland. As I get older, I try not to sit on boards and to do projects.

My Advice

- Plan what the other activities you are going to do.
- Challenge yourself.
- Be involved in life, whether it's volunteering, service clubs, or other activities.
- Keep involved.

Name: Ken Goldman
Occupation: CFO, Yahoo
Retirement Age: Not Retired
Current Age: 67
Protirement Activities: **Not Retired/Gradually Retiring**; Health Enthusiast; **Family Enthusiast**

My Protirement Story

I don't think, in today's world, there is a set age to retire anymore. When I joined Yahoo, I felt it would be for four to five years, but I would play it by ear and see how it went. I wasn't fixated about when I would retire. I watch other folks, in other companies, who are 70 and older, who haven't retired and they are thriving, so I don't have a fixed perspective on retiring. The best example of that is Warren Buffet, who had an annual meeting recently. He is 86 and Charlie Munger is 93. Many of their board members are in their 80s.

I think it's more important to ensure you have great health. If you are healthy and able to manage your time in a way that works for you, you will have free time to do other things, in addition to work. I don't think you have to have a fixed time to retire. We'll see what's best for me after Yahoo, but I could see another CFO job down the road.

The two things I would like to get better at are wind surfing and kite sailing. I have been learning how to kite sail. We will be spending some time kiting in Maui this summer. I also want to learn to play golf better. All of our kids are in their 20s, two of them live here and one of them lives in New York. As I get older, I want to spend more time with them, as well.

I have two avocations that I want to pursue. Also, I will spend more time working out. Another thing I will do in my free time is read more. I am a prolific reader—when I have time. I am a big believer in reading and learning, especially about business. Those activities will keep me occupied.

I am also on a number of public and private boards, and plan to dedicate more of my time to helping on those. I have become a better board member by being in the game as a CFO.

I like to be occupied and very busy. I get antsy if I am not fully occupied.

My Advice

- Figure out what you do well and do it.
- Figure out what you enjoy doing and do it.
- Have balance in life.

- Have time for family.
- Stay in good shape physically.

Name: Dr. Kwame D.
Occupation: Pediatrician
Retirement Age: Not Retired/Gradually Retiring
Current Age: 73
Protirement Activities: **Not Retired/Gradually Retiring;** Hobbyist; Community Builder; Health Enthusiast; Philanthropist; Family Enthusiast

My Protirement Story

For me, a key to work is you have to love your job. If you don't love your job, you shouldn't be doing it. I love coming to work, I love doing what I do, my brain is still working, I am still good at it. So, at the age of 65, retirement wasn't on the table at all. I now work four days a week and take Wednesdays off for myself.

At 70, I was still doing great. I am still passing my college exams every two years, so as long as I am still doing it well, I do not plan on retiring. I read a lot and usually have two books on the go at a time. In 2012, I got really sick and had to have major surgery. That set me back a bit, so I don't play tennis or squash anymore, which is tough. I had to readjust. I now go to the gym and do my thing, but had to readjust my workouts.

In retirement, I will continue to do things I am passionate about and to advocate for people, especially back home. When I do eventually retire, I plan on going to Ghana to work at the hospital. I will also travel, invest, do charity work, and be involved in politics.

My Advice

- You really should not retire from life. Studies are quite clear, if you retire, stay at home, drink beer all day, you will die early. We know that.
- Always keep doing something.

- Always be honest with yourself and with others, as much as you can. Be your own critic.
- Help others.
- Do something that you love. When you love something, there is no need to retire, you can modify it if you want, but you don't need to stop completely.
- Pay attention to your health. When I was sick a few years ago, I recovered quickly because of my fitness.
- There are 5 F's that I think we all need to work on in our older life to be happy: Fitness, Faith, Family, Finances, and Friends.

Photo:
Dean Marrantz

Name: Liona Boyd
Occupation: Musician
Retirement Age: Not Retired
Current Age: 68
Protirement Activities: **Not Retired/Gradually Retiring**

My Protirement Story

I have been lucky that my work, really, is my hobby; is my passion, my love. It never really seemed like work. Years later, I got musician's focal dystonia by overpracticing. I had to quit for six years, so I guess I did retire, for those years. It was heartbreaking for me. I had a taste of early retirement and it was miserable. Gradually, I did retrain my fingers. I'm still not up to doing complex concertos, but I don't want to; that part of my life is over.

I went through a very difficult summer in 2016. I fell and shattered my shoulder and my knee in Palm Beach, Florida. After a week in the hospital, I did a month of rehab in Toronto. That was a very difficult time .

I had a taste of what it's like to be unable to play guitar, twice, and now I'm very grateful. Every time I step on the stage, I think how lucky I am. I still do classical technique and the odd classical piece, but basically, I've morphed, reinvented myself into a singer-songwriter. But classical guitar is still the basis of my music even though I've always loved lyrics and words.

I'll probably always be writing; I have a new album and a new autobiography that were just released, They are both called *No Remedy for Love*, from a quote by David Henry Thoreau: "There's no remedy for love but to love more," which I find quite profound. I wrote that song dedicated to Leonard Cohen.

Sometimes I do feel lonely because I sense my mortality. Prince Philip said to me, "Once you start sensing your mortality, then you have to make some changes in your life."

Last fall I recorded with Rompin' Ronnie Hawkins; he's a legend. He and his wife invited us to go over to his "Hawkstone" manor. He sang on a tribute song I wrote to Gordon Lightfoot. I decided Gordon, who really helped launch my career, deserved a song. I got permission from the publishers to use some of his lines. I've combined a whole lot of his different songs. Any Lightfoot fan will recognize the lines right away. The chorus: "Lightfoot, Lightfoot, your songs will live forevermore / Lightfoot, Lightfoot, our Canadian troubadour." Ronnie learned the lines. They're good pals, they love each other.

My Advice

- People should always have a variety of things going on in their lives.
- Don't be narrow.
- Be individual, and don't just follow the crowd.
- Don't give up; you've got to keep going, keep trying.

Name: The Honorable Rob Nicholson
Occupation: Federal Politician
Retirement Age: Not Retired
Current Age: 65
Protirement Activities: **Not Retired/Gradually Retiring**

My Protirement Story

I have had a great work life and enjoyed my career wherever I found myself. I will be 67 at the end of this term of government. I am not ready for retirement at this time and currently plan to run again in the next federal election, but will make a final decision when we are closer to that date.

I believe the trick to being successful in retirement is to be doing something that will satisfy you. You can be making a positive difference wherever you are in life. When my first opportunity to represent the Niagara Falls riding as the Member of Parliament ended in 1993 I was leaving a Cabinet position as the Minister of Science and Minister Responsible for Small Business and had to get back into my former career practicing law. During an interview about a month later I was asked about what it was like to be out of politics. The reporter wanted to know if I had taken on many new responsibilities. I told her the truth; they asked me to be Secretary of the men's club at my Church. She said "Do you think this is a little bit of a come down?" and I replied that it wasn't the only thing I would be doing. I was also going back to practicing law.

You have to believe that wherever you are, you are making a difference. You are making a contribution and however you are doing that you can be satisfied. I think something like community volunteering would be very satisfying for me once I do retire; anything where I can make a contribution to the community.

I had a grandmother who lived to be 101 and I noticed she was always looking forward to the next thing in her life; she was looking forward to going to the next graduation of her 27 grand children, or the next wedding. She didn't spend a lot of time talking about how it was in the past. I always thought to myself that that was one of the secrets of living fully in your retirement, always looking forward.

My Advice

- Get involved with different groups in the community.
- Have some sort of plan.

- Continue to interact with people to maintain your relationships and be a part of something where you feel you are making a difference, making a contribution.

Name:	Ronnie Hawkins
Occupation:	Musician
Retirement Age:	Not Retired/Gradually Retiring
Current Age:	81
Protirement Activities:	**Not Retired/Gradually Retiring**

My Protirement Story

I'm 81. I've got a good band now; top-of-the-line musicians. They're in three or four different groups. They're great musicians, so it only takes a week of practice before a gig.

They did a show where I did five songs in the night. It was called: "An Intimate Night with Ronnie Hawkins." We did several shows like that. It's me just answering questions about rock 'n' roll, just like I'm telling you now. And I had guest artists; three or four guest artists that sang, and then I did about five songs. We did several shows with that. That's what they're wanting us to do now.

I could've retired, I was working so hard and making money, at 50 years old, but I let my lawyer and my management company talk me into one last project and they completely broke me. They ended up with everything. I thought they were my friends. But that happens in showbiz; money turns people funny.

I got to work all these extra years. If I had a choice I'd have played forever. Well, I'm still playing. I'm cutting stuff with Gordon Lightfoot, Kris Kristofferson, and Willie Nelson; and we have a record coming out, the three of us, called *Me and Bobby McGee*.

Sometime my story's going to end. I don't know the ending yet. A film crew came in to film me. They were going to come for six weeks because the doctors only gave me six weeks or less to live. CTV sent a film crew in to do a documentary. We got the lights and everything set up and they followed me everywhere I went. I said "Well, I'm dying; I'm going to go out like a rocket."

I brought in all these musician friends of mine and we played. But I didn't die and I went back for that last body-scan. The tumor, the cancer in my pancreas, was growing. The film crews were getting a little nervous, staying here that long. Then, I took that last scan and the tumor was completely gone; it had disappeared. Nobody had ever done that. They filmed the doctors saying they can't believe this; it's some kind of a miracle. But it upset the film crew because now they had to change the ending of the documentary. They called it *Still Alive and Kicking,* instead of *Dead and Gone*. They filmed me playing after I came back. It won an award for documentary of the year.

My Advice

- Do what you are happy doing!

Name:	Roy McMurtry
Occupation:	Lawyer, Politician
Retirement Age:	Not Retired
Current Age:	84
Protirement Activities:	**Not Retired/Gradually Retiring**; Hobbyist; Community Builder; Family Enthusiast

My Protirement Story

After my retirement as Chief Justice of Ontario in 2007, I joined a large law firm, Gowlings LLP, and worked there for about seven years, before I came to Hull & Hull, LLP. The founder of the firm was one of my closest friends, the late Rodney Hull. His son, Ian, now manages the firm. He is my son, Harry's, closest friend.

Harry has been fighting Parkinson's disease for fourteen years. He walked five hundred miles from his home in New York City to raise money for Parkinson's. He raised almost a million dollars.

I prepared two major public policy reports for the Ontario government, after retiring as a judge, one being after the shooting death of the fifteen-year-old, Jordan Manners, in a local high school. The Premier, Dalton McGuinty, asked me to chair a committee to study: "The Roots of Youth Violence in Ontario." The Attorney General, Michael Bryant, also asked me to do a report on a review of the Criminal Injuries Compensation Board in Ontario at about the same time.

I am still oil painting during the summer and particularly on weekends.

I'm on various committees, volunteer work that is *pro bono*. I was Chancellor of York University for six years. I presided over 280 convocations over those six years, and according to the university, shook 65,000 hands.

My Advice

- Keep busy. Health-wise, people pay a price by not keeping active.
- Pursue volunteerism, give back.

Name:	Sally M.
Occupation:	Real Estate Broker
Retirement Age:	Not Retired
Current Age:	65
Protirement Activities:	**Not Retired/Gradually Retiring;** Travel Enthusiast

My Protirement Story

To be honest, I do not think of retiring and I do not believe that there is any set age anymore for retiring. It used to be that 65 was that magic number everyone looked forward to, or were forced into. I know a lot of people who retired in their 40's and 50's and I also know a number who are still working in their 70's and 80's, because they are able to and want to. I think retirement is now a state of mind, rather than age.

At one point I thought that 55 would be the ideal age to retire. Then 55 came and went, and so did the thought of stopping work. I think though, we eventually get to a stage where our life and work balance is more of a blend. What was, or is, work becomes a real part of who we are, and a part of our life happening events.

I am extremely active in my work life and my personal life. I am not in a 9 to 5 type of job and face totally different situations every day. I get very involved in people's lives and at times this "job" can be very life consuming, and at the same time, very life fulfilling.

I firmly believe that remaining in the work world, and being engaged, is very good for the mind, body and soul. My roles do change a little over the years and we all tend to get repurposed throughout our life time.

My Advice

- Enjoy whatever you are doing and whatever that may be
- Stay healthy, physically and mentally by being active and engaged
- Do not think that there is a set date to retire...think of the different stages of continuation of life
- Enjoy life and all the life happening events.
- Life happens as we are living it, so pay attention

CHAPTER 6: PROTIREMENT CATEGORY #2: CONTINGENCY WORKERS

"Protired Baby Boomers are the new face of the Contingent Economy. They include the: Part-time Contractors; On-Call Substitutors; and Project Work Freelancers."
Ellis Katsof

Introduction

As the economy began to rebound from the 2008 financial crisis, companies moved toward smaller workforces and only increased their workforces when larger projects or contracts were obtained. This has created a new group of workers called, "Contingency Workers." The Contingency Worker is employed on a contract basis. They do not have an implicit or explicit contract for ongoing employment. They include Part-Time Contractors, On-Call Substitutes, and Project Work Freelancers.

Facts about "Contingency Workers"

I call the first category of Contingency Workers the "Part-Time Contractors." They are often hired on a part-time basis to increase staffing during peak periods of the year. Baby Boomers who pursue these positions are usually interested in working but not interested in pursuing 52-week a year positions. This gives them time to pursue other interests during the slow periods.

Harold's work in his son's store is an example of a Part-Time Contractor. Harold, 86 years old, used to own and operate the men's wear store. After retiring 10 years ago, Harold has returned to work at the store three days a week, but is free to travel as he pleases throughout the year because of the flexibility of the part-time nature of his work.

The second category is the "On-Call Substitutors." They are hired on a shift basis and are usually on an On-Call list to back-fill ill or vacationing employees. The On-Call Substitutors are often found in professional settings where a minimum staffing level is required and vacant staff positions must be filled. Hospital nurses, drug store pharmacists, nursing home attendants, and teachers are examples of these types of positions. Doctors fill locums for other doctors when they are ill or on an extended leave of absence. I consider these a type of On-Call Substitutor, as well, because they are filling in for the absent physician rather than doing a special project.

Kevin retired from his practice as a family physician when he was 65, but since that time, has filled in for other physicians and completed 10 locums over the years. This has given him the time to travel, teach medical students at a local university, pursue his photography hobby, read, and sing in a local choir.

The third category includes "Project Work Freelancers." When Baby Boomers retire, they often have certain knowledge and expertise that make it very attractive for former employers to hire them back to complete specific projects. These are time limited projects that allow Baby Boomers to still pursue other activities during their Protirement.

Elco retired when he was 58. As CEO for a large corporation, he was asked to return numerous times over a four-year period to complete special projects for the firm. Maurice, a banker who retired when he was 58, was asked to return to the banking industry to help retirees, who were turning 71, convert their retirement savings into retirement income plans. He was able to work at times that were convenient to him and his active protired lifestyle. He did this for about seven more years.

"Contingency Workers" Protirement Stories

Five of the people interviewed had participated in Contingency Worker activities. All five individuals also participated in other Protirement activities, such as: New Careers, Care Givers, Hobbyists, Travel Enthusiasts, Community Building, Writers/Performers, and Health Enthusiasts.

"Contingency Worker" personal Protirement Stories follow.

Name: Elco D.
Occupation: Corporate Executive
Retirement Age: 58
Current Age: 70
Protirement Activities: **Contingency Worker;** Caregiver; Hobbyist; **Travel Enthusiast; Community Builder**

My Protirement Story

I thought I wouldn't retire until I was 70 or 75, but I was battling chronic fatigue, work had become very stressful, and I had no life outside of work. After a discussion with my wife, we decided it wasn't worth it. So, in 2004, after 40 years, I retired at the age of 58.

After retirement, my wife and I got on a plane and flew to Vancouver. We took a cruise to Alaska and then rented an SUV in Vancouver and drove to Calgary. We stayed away for four weeks.

I did no planning prior to retirement. I struggled for about a year after retirement. It took about a year to get work out of my system. During that time, I did a lot of work on projects around the house. After a year or so, I began volunteering, and it has been very rewarding. Also, for 3½ years following my retirement, the company brought me back for special projects.

My wife and I do a lot of things together, but we also give each other space to do our own things. We have never felt that we were in each other's space before we retired, and that has continued since we each retired.

I have to give back to the community for what it has given to my mother and brother when they needed support. After about a year, I received a phone call from the Alzheimer's Society of Niagara. They asked me to join the Board of Directors, which I did for six years. Eventually, I served on the Alzheimer Ontario Board for six years.

After six years, I wanted to get involved with mental health issues because we were dealing with mental health issues with my brother. I became a Board member at Pathstone Mental Health. I have been on the board for seven years and am now the Chair of the Board.

Gardening has always been fun and kept me outdoors. We downsized our home from two story to a bungalow town house. There will be less regular maintenance without our pool or large garden to care for. It's with mixed emotions; moving from our large home, but we couldn't continue with the work load of gardening.

Caregiving has also been a very big part of my retirement years, for my brother who had mental health challenges, for a sister-in-law who has Alzheimer's, a brother-in-law who had dementia, and two nieces who have cancer.

We love travelling. Since my retirement, we have gone on about 30 cruises. We have been to Antarctica, Galapagos Islands, Europe, Caribbean, and Vancouver to Tokyo. Our plan is to go to the Baltic's in the near future.

My Advice

- Stay involved and do something worthwhile, whether it is volunteering, hobbies, or other things that are important to you.

Name:	Harold N.
Occupation:	Business Owner
Retirement Age:	76 – Began working part-time
Current Age:	86
Protirement Activities:	**Contingency Worker**; Hobbyist; **Community Builder**

My Protirement Story

I played tennis until I turned 80, when I decided that my knees couldn't do it anymore. These days, instead of playing tennis, I now play bridge, two or three nights a week. I am very involved in the Synagogue. I was its president 30 years ago, and am currently the President again. I was also chair of the Chevra Kadisha and the bingo fund raiser. I also work three days a week at the family store my son now operates.

My Advice

- Make sure they have something else in the pipeline to do or else don't retire.
- Have a plan that lets you do some of the things you couldn't do when you were working, but that you would like to do.
- Don't cut yourself off entirely from business or what you were doing.

Name:	John H.
Occupation:	Executive, Department of Fisheries & Oceans
Retirement Age:	57
Current Age:	64
Protirement Activities:	**Contingency Work;** Hobbyist; Community Builder; **Performer**

My Protirement Story

I decided to retire early after 32 years of professional service. I left when I was 57. I had a delayed reaction. My wife and I went on a trip to Florida. I wanted to have some kind of activity. I wasn't able to continue playing basketball at the level that I was playing, so as my body got older I took up golf. I really enjoyed my first year of retirement. My wife was still working and our kids were pretty much gone.

That fall, around Christmastime, I was doing theatre and was president of the theatre organization but I became depressed. It was something new; I had never experienced that before. My wife is a psychiatric nurse and she knew what it was right away, but I was totally taken aback by it.

Looking back, I realize that it was, more than anything, because I had just stopped doing anything physical after golf was over. I wasn't a member of a gym, which I'd always done. I hadn't taken up any other interests.

I was very fortunate that my wife was there. We went to my doctor and worked it through. It took me a while, but once we figured out what it was, I came to grips with it and got the help that I needed. I realized that I had to have some structure in terms of my physical activity. I joined the gym and went regularly. I walked and, when golf season came back, I began playing again.

The next year we travelled again and I did more theatre. I made a conscious decision to have more structure. During that time, I also started getting calls from my former colleagues, asking me if I would get involved in some projects. I went back to work part-time. I was asked to write a small book on the lobster industry. I did some human resources work. That helped me a lot; it was stimulating, good for my brain, and engaged me.

At the same time, I needed to set some goals. As a New Year's resolution, I said, "These are two things I want to do." One was starting to paint again, and the other was to play music again. One day a month, I invited people who also liked music to my house and we started learning to play Irish sessions. Now, we do it once a week instead of once a month.

We began playing Irish sessions at a new local pub every Sunday. We eventually added Scottish music, as well. We applied for a grant from a local community foundation and produced a CD. We sell it and donate the profits to the local food bank. We've raised $7,000 so far.

I also started painting last year and painted Christmas presents for family. I also did another project for the province of Nova Scotia on lobster. This year, I got a call and was asked to help with developing some advice to federal legal services on a court case.

Keeping your brain active and keeping your body active are really important.

My Advice

- Make sure you really want to retire.
- Find ways to be active regularly.
- You need daily structure that includes physical activity, good nourishment, and mental stimulation.

Name:	Kevin F.
Occupation:	Family Physician
Retirement Age:	65
Current Age:	72
Protirement Activities:	**Contingency Worker; New Career;** Hobbyist; Travel Enthusiast; Family Enthusia

My Protirement Story

My dad was dead at 72. I knew that I might have a limited time and I wasn't sure what else I wanted to do. I had hip surgery at 65 and felt it might be a time to stop. You could easily stay in my business for ever and a lot of people do. When I turned 65, there was no way I felt 65 or acted 65. Sometimes, I feel like I need to start acting my age. You have to continue and do stuff.

I loved my job. I ran into someone from the McMaster Medical program who asked me if I wanted to teach in the medical program. I taught professional competencies and mental health behavioral science. I began with a two-year contract, extended it for two more years, and finally extended it for one more two-year term. I will be finished a year from now in the spring of 2017. I enjoyed it but it ended up interfering with my other retirement activities because I always had to be there for the classes, and read all their essays and do their evaluations.

We have travelled a lot across Europe. We go to California in November and March for golf. Although golf is fun, I prefer to go for a walk in the desert to take pictures of rocks. I love photography and have done it since 1970, when my wife gave me a wonderful camera.

We visit our grandchildren and children whenever we can. Occasionally I take photography courses. I have done short-term and long-term locums in about 10 different offices since I retired. I am now going to stop doing locums.

I got into a choir recently. They are so lovely, it's so much fun. We are just there to enjoy the music. We sing at retirement homes. I really enjoy it.

My best man at my wedding now has dementia. It's the saddest thing. You have to keep active. I read a lot of stuff and I am never bored. We had a larger house up on the hill for 35 years and moved down here to a smaller house five years ago.

As I age/grow I am increasingly aware of my good fortune. I am very grateful to have this life, in this country, at this time.

My Advice

- You have to do something that amuses you, something that's interesting even if it doesn't pay well, something that involves people.
- You have to keep people in the equation, stay involved.
- I find I value family more as i go along in this life.
- Laugh, keep your sense of humor.

Name: Lloyd Robertson
Occupation: National Broadcaster
Retirement Age: 77
Current Age: 83
Protirement Activities: **Contingency Worker;** Community Builder; Writer/Performer; Health Enthusiast

My Protirement Story

I happily stepped aside from the nightly news when I turned 77. CTV was very good, and immediately asked, "Is there anything else you would like to do?" I had already been hosting on W5 and doing some longer reports for the show, so they said, "Why not take a slightly larger role?" I said that I didn't want to crowd out anybody else, but would like to continue contributing if I could, so they gave me the title of Chief Correspondent. I hosted and did four or five reports a year for W5, before stepping aside in 2016 to make room for Kevin Newman, who is now the program's Managing Editor. I'm still working as a Special Correspondent for CTV News, contributing to news specials along with occasional items for W5. It keeps me in the game, it keeps me active. I find that when I am into a story, the adrenalin flows and I enjoy it. But I don't want to be too tied down. I want a lot of this new time for trips with my wife, Nancy, who watched me work every night of the week for 41 years, and for grandchildren and those other enjoyable and reflective periods the senior years can bring.

When I first retired, it was a huge relief, not having to be *on* every day. That lasted for a month or so and then I began to tune into the news more regularly, and occasionally felt I missed being around for those big stories. However, I knew that I had to adjust and, gradually, I weaned myself off the daily rush. Fortunately, as noted, I was able to come back and make contributions. For example, on election night, I had great fun sitting on the desk as a commentator, still in the middle of the action, but not having to anchor the broadcast with the enormous responsibilities that job entails.

Shortly before I was about to retire from the daily news, an interesting proposal dropped into my lap and it meant the immediate post-news period would be very busy in a different way. Michael Levine, an agent I had known for years, called me about doing a book. It was something others had encouraged and I'd been mulling over. Levine said if I was ever going to do it, now was the time. I had some hesitation but finally decided to go ahead. In my exploratory discussions about the book, I talked to my old buddy Craig Oliver. He said, "If you're going to write it you have to be honest and tell people who you really are." I told him that's fine, but that would mean talking about my mother's mental illness, and how it affected my growing up in Stratford, Ontario, the huge stigma that surrounded it, my mother's prefrontal lobotomy operation …the whole thing. He said, "If you're serious about writing a memoir that reflects your life, you've got to do it" So, I ploughed ahead and we got the book out by October 2012.

What really surprised me when I was going across Canada on the book tour was all the questions about mental health, just one question after another. People came forward and said that they had had the same problems in their own families. It struck me that we had hit a chord. For some time after the book came out, I was often called upon to speak on mental health issues to interested groups across the country.

I am very aware of giving back and I try to do that as much as I can. I am involved in the Stratford Perth County Community Foundation. My wife and I have helped to start up an arm of that fund that supports young people who are disadvantaged in one way or another, as I was when I was a kid. My family was poor and my mother had those mental health issues, but I got lucky, I found my escape in the wonderful world of radio and went on to make it a career in broadcasting. Other kids may not be so fortunate and they need a hand up. That's what our fund is about.

I also try to keep physically active. I walk and try to run every once in a while, if the legs allow it. And Pilates is helping to keep me limbered up. Keeping the mind active is also important through reading, continuing to work occasionally, volunteering, and, in my case, playing Scrabble, that kind of stuff.

I think if you have to keep doing things, you can't let your mind and body ossify.

I have seen people stop living after they retire. They become depressed, morose, inactive, drink too much, and within a couple of years end up dead. It is so important to remain active in one way or another after you retire. It doesn't matter what you do as long as you're out there and participating in life. If people choose to go to seed, that's their business, of course, but it's sad; you leave others behind who hoped to have you around for a while longer.

My Advice

- Keep active, physically and mentally.
- Always *want to* participate in life.

CHAPTER 7: PROTIREMENT CATEGORY #3: NEW CAREERS/JOBS

"Is it time to define what is most important to you, and choose the career that fits you perfectly?"
Unknown

Introduction

In their Protirement, Boomers are embracing new careers, some for additional income and others to keep busy. They also start new jobs or careers to feel good about themselves and to have new challenges. New Careers/Jobs are sometimes closely linked to previous careers or jobs, but can also be in totally different areas.

Facts about "New Careers/Jobs"

Repurposing skills that have already been highly developed in previous careers, allow people to move between sectors and into new jobs. For example, a common move today is repurposing corporate skills to assist people in applying their skills in the not-for-profit sector.

New Careers/Jobs can either be full-time or part-time ventures. Some people go back to school to complete training programs to help them transition into new careers. Others learn experientially as they are trained on the job.

New job recruitment and placement organizations are sprouting up to match the protired Baby Boomer looking for work with employers who are interested in hiring them. Examples include: Boomers Work (Canada) and Seniors Job Bank (USA). There are many online placement services in the USA serving this population, as well. Some of them include: RetiredBrains.com, YourEncore.com, and The Encore Fellowships Network.

New Careers/Jobs

There are numerous articles on the web highlighting the type of work that retirees pursue, ranging from professional white collar careers to skilled blue collar jobs, as well as part-time jobs like school crossing guards, courtesy car drivers, and store clerks. A sampling of these articles include: *Jobs for Seniors: What are the Best Jobs After Retirement? (New Retirement.com), 10 Best Jobs for retirees (HowStuffWorks.com)' and Part-Time Jobs for Retirees (AARP).* In Protirement, there are no "right" careers or jobs, only those that meet the personal needs that drive each individual to keep busy. As identified in Chapter 3, these personal needs include:

- a purpose;
- a sense of identity;
- increasing self-worth;
- a routine and structure to daily life;
- intellectual stimulation;
- social interaction; and/or
- additional income.

"New Careers/Jobs" Protirement Stories

I interviewed a wide age range of people from 55 to 83 years old who pursued New Careers or Jobs in their Protirement. One protired when he was 31; three of them protired between the ages of 50 and 59, while six protired between the age of 60 and 68. Three are between the ages of 62 and 69. Five are in their 70s and two are in their 80s. They are all enjoying their protired careers or jobs with no immediate plans to stop being active.

They were also involved in numerous other Protirement activities, such as: Seniorpreneurs, Care Givers, Hobbyists, Travel Enthusiasts, Community Builders, Health Enthusiasts, and Life Long Learners.

Edited versions of their personal Protirement Stories follow.

Name: Alvin Curling
Occupation: MPP, Cabinet Minister
Retirement Age: 65
Current Age: 76
Protirement Activities: **New Career/Job**; Community Builder

My Protirement Story

Prime Minister Paul Martin called me after I announced my retirement, and said, "I would like to appoint you as Ambassador to the Dominican Republic." I was 65 at the time and said I was planning on leaving public life. I thought about it. There were two friends and mentors I have had throughout my career: Keith Davey, who was my Campaign Manager and a personal friend. The other person was Roy McMurtry. They both said to me, "You don't say NO to a Prime Minister." I realized they were right. I said yes to the Prime Minister and spent 2½ years in that role.

I feel that retirement has been a journey. We learned about our 5 senses; touch, taste, feel, sight, and sound. There is a soul about it all, the intuition or karma. I am in touch with that process more now since retiring.

Farmers don't retire. They plant, and plant, and plant, and harvest in between. And then there is a big harvest. I am in the harvesting stage now. Harvesting is the soul that I am talking about. When I speak to people I have this "wow." I am reaping from what I have sown over the years of understanding humanity. I don't suffer from anxiety anymore. When I was working, there was an anxiety. I planted many things over the years, some grew and others didn't. Through experience, I have learned not to worry about it.

The harvesting is now what is important, it is a different focus. The phone has not stopped, it is easier for people to say, "Do you have time, come and do this." I am in "retirement" but I am quite busy. I am assisting the Caribbean on airport security. Visual Defense is a company that I am involved with. I am introducing and engaging them with Jamaica, Barbados, and Dominican Republic. I am also trying also to assist, support, and mentor young people in Jamaica and Canada.

The path of harvesting involves helping when people ask. For example, I sit on the Scarborough Hospital Caribbean Philanthropic Club. Another example was when a young man called me up and said he wanted to put my name forward for a new school to be named in my honour, the Alvin Curling Public School. Talk about reaping! It's a wonderful school. Then another young person, who I mentored, asked me if she could put my name forward to get a street in my name.

My Advice

- Whatever you do; do it well.
- Don't let anyone define you.
- Happiness brings good health.
- You will be whatever you will be.
- The danger of talking about retirement is talking about stopping. Keep being active.
- Retirement is the time to harvest, to reap.

Name:	Bob L.
Occupation:	Hospital Executive
Retirement Age:	56
Current Age:	74
Protirement Activities:	**New Career/Job**; Community Builder

My Protirement Story

It was never my intention to retire early, but due to the merging of all of the hospitals in the region, I decided to "jump before I was shoved." I was 56 at the time.

I felt I was too young to retire, so I went into financial planning with a small firm in Niagara. I also volunteered at a board level and am hands on at a few non-profit agencies. A member of one of the agencies approached me to review the administration at a small not for profit agency. In 2001, after making the necessary changes to the organization, the board offered me the position as Executive Director; I have been there ever since—16 years.

My Advice:

- Keep active.
- With a guaranteed income (pension), you have many more choices, you can take a position with less pay, less stress, but which still gets you out the door every day.
- Plan for retirement, money is one issue, but equally as important is what you are going to do with your free time.
- Everyone needs some structure to their days; develop a structure that works for you.

Name:	Chris B.
Occupation:	Steel industry Executive, Financial Planner
Retirement Age:	68
Current Age:	74
Protirement Activities:	**New Career/Job;** Community Builder

My Protirement Story

In 2007, I joined with another financial planner who was fully incorporated. Over the next three years, I handed over my clients to her. It was a good succession plan. In 2010, my health wasn't good and I was pretty tired at the end of the day. I was 68 and thought it was a good time to retire.

My wife, Ann, had retired earlier and had always done the lion's share of the housework. I was trying to figure out my role! It took a little while to make the adjustment. It was a challenge but it wasn't acrimonious. Over time, we sorted out how to share the house in a new way. But the kitchen is still her domain, thank goodness! She cooks and I set the table and clean up. My wife and I just celebrated our 50th anniversary and are blessed with a wonderful marriage.

After three months of 'retirement' with my health improving, I was looking for things to do and began networking through my Rotary club. I went to see a Rotarian friend who I had worked with in the past. Through Rotary, I met with another Rotarian who had heard about my interests through the grapevine. She motioned me to a chair and said, "You are hired." I said, "What do you want me to do?" For five years, I worked part-time for her, promoting the local Community Foundation.

About two years ago, through the Foundation, I began helping charities set up their own Planned Giving programs.

My Advice

- Make sure you have something lined up to do when you retire. Do not retire cold turkey. The novelty will run out in six weeks, and then what are you going to do?
- You have to have a purpose in life when you retire.
- Be very sensitive to the roles with your partner before your retirement, and don't try to change them very quickly.

Name: Garry B.
Occupation: Educator
Retirement Age: 54
Current Age: 62
Protirement Activities: **New Career/Job;** Travel Enthusiast; Life Long Learner; Family Enthusiast

My Protirement Story

I retired when I was 54. I loved teaching but hated the political action. I had the chance to retire, so I took it. I knew too many people in teaching that had retired and either died very quickly in the first few years or had stayed too late, hated teaching, and became very bitter. I loved teaching and didn't want to leave hating it.

First thing I did when I retired was renovations of the cottage. We had planned to add onto the cottage and I went into construction like a mad man because I'm handy. By the end of October, we completed the addition.

I started working out at this fitness club in January. I loved meeting 900 people a day at school and suddenly there was just me. The social aspect of being a member at the gym is terrific. The social interaction was one thing that the club gave me. I really enjoyed the exercise but the social interaction was also terrific.

One of the trainers from the club was teaching a personal training course at Niagara College, so I took the course. I hadn't intended to be a personal trainer. I just wanted the personal knowledge. It comes from being a lifelong learner. She then suggested that I become a trainer at the fitness club. I have been a personal trainer for 12 years. I work part-time and also write for the club's magazine, which gives me the chance to use my creative writing skills.

CanFit Pro is the Canadian professional governing body for personal trainers. It holds a big annual conference in Toronto. I volunteered for two years and was then asked to be a Team Leader for registration. I have done this for over eight years.

One of my sons got a job in Georgia, and in April I took off by myself to visit him. It was the first time I ever travelled by myself.

I used to tell my wife, "Don't mess with my schedule." The first day she retired, I came home from the club at about 10 in the morning and she had already done the laundry. She sat down with me and said, "Now what are we going to do?" There was no "we" for over 30 years. We left the house every morning and we wouldn't see each other until 4 or 5 o'clock in the afternoon. That seemed to have worked for 30 years so why change it now?

Travelling is also a big thing for me. We go south every February. I usually do the beach, walk, run, and read a lot, as well as just relax. We have been in to Eastern Europe. We have been to China, Ireland, Peru, England, Scotland, Wales, and France. I'd like to go to Iceland and the Galapagos Islands.

My Advice

- Have something to do, find something you love to do.
- Consider what you like about your job and see if you can replicate that in your retirement.
- Don't save your money until you're too old to spend it.

Name: John M.
Occupation: City Administrator
Retirement Age: 58
Current Age: 65
Protirement Activities: **New Career/Job;** Community Builder; Health Enthusiast; Life Long Learner

My Protirement Story

Once I decided that I was going to retire, I was presented with several employment opportunities, in both the private and public sector. However I had made a conscious decision not to continue to do the same type of work that I had been involved for the past 36 years. Because of my lifelong involvement in the Church, I had often thought that someday I might work in a Church or for a Christian organization. At the time I did retired there were a lot of changes occurring in the Anglican Church of Canada, which I had been a member for for most of my life.

As fate would have it, a priest who was involved in the Anglican movement approached me. He explained that due to the changes in the Canadian church a new organization was being formed. This organization didn't want to remain under the authority of the Anglican Church of Canada, but did want to remain faithful to the Anglican tradition. It's now called the

Anglican Network of Canada. I took a two-year contract to set up the governance model for the new Church. By the time I got involved, we had about five parishes. We now have approximately 70 parishes across Canada.

At that time, I indicated that I wasn't interested in being involved in the operation of the organization but would help with the governance issues. That was 7½ years ago and now governance is well established. My role has evolved and now I am the National Director, which unfortunately includes the oversight for all operations.

With a second career, I had no intention of going to work at an office every day. I now go to an office in Burlington two days and work from home for the balance of the week. I am very motivated by learning, so this job continues to be very attractive because there is so much to learn.

I still play hockey two mornings a week in the winter and ride my bike as much as possible through the summer. I am a member of a gym and work out almost daily. I am also a volunteer with the local health system and currently serve as Chair of the board. As well, I have chaired their Strategic Planning Committee. I have also maintained a leadership role in my own church.

I have three grandchildren and they continue to take up a lot of my time.

My wife and I also like to travel and we will take two or three trips a year of various durations.

My Advice

- Stay engaged with the community.
- Always be thinking about developing skill sets that can be used throughout your life.
- Remember the importance of interacting with people.
- Family is a priority.

Name:	Honorable Ken Dryden
Occupation:	Hockey Player
Retirement Age:	31
Current Age:	69
Protirement Activities:	**New Careers; Political Activist;** Hobbyist; Travel Enthusiast, **Writer**

My Protirement Story

When I retired from hockey, I felt that was my real retirement. I've retired once in my life, and that was when I was 31 years old. It was a full retirement, with all of the same kind of experiences that one has when you retire at an older age. In fact, the actual feeling of retirement—and I remember vividly—is that my formal retirement came in July, when the announcement was made. That's when I retired, except, when I retired, I thought, "Oh well, this was kind of a tough day because I really liked what I was doing, but felt it was time to do something else." It didn't feel that bad; it didn't feel as bad as I thought it would feel.

The summer went on and then the fall began. Training camp began in September, and that's when I realized that I *really was* retired. When the next season begins and it begins without you, it finally sinks in that you are really retired. If you're working in an office, you don't retire on the Friday; you retire on the Monday when you don't go back. I was quite overwhelmed by the depth of the feeling that I felt in September. It was… "Ah-hah, right, that's what this is."

The question was, "What next?" In the summer of '79, after I retired, I decided that I was going to take the bar course, and I was pretty sure I was going to write a book. But even if I did both of those things, there would be an "after that." I thought, "What I'd like to do, really, is think about the most interesting jobs in the country, and who seem to be the most interesting people in the country. I would talk to them and see if I could be hired as their assistant."

The following year, I took my bar course, which in Ontario was almost a like a full university academic year. It started in September and finished at the end of March. It was offered in Ottawa for the first time, so we moved to Ottawa. I took the bar course and my bar exams.

At the same time, ABC asked me if I would be a color commentator for the Olympics in 1980, which were in Lake Placid. I did some pre-Olympic work; I went to Moscow right around Christmas for a pre-Olympic competition. I went to Lake Placid for a period of about a month and would commute back to Ottawa to take my exams. I was doing that while I was doing my Lake Placid commentating job.

When that was over, I wanted to write a book. I had read lots of sports books in my life; I liked reading sports books. Some were really good, but even the best ones didn't quite describe my experiences. I decided I wanted to write a book myself, I didn't want a ghostwriter.

We stayed in Ottawa until our daughter was finished school for the year. We thought that a book could be written pretty much anywhere so why not be somewhere other than Montreal, Ottawa, or Toronto. Our kids were young enough, our daughter was four, turning five, and our son was two. We thought, "Well, where would be an interesting place to live?" We talked to a number of people and decided to live in Cambridge, England.

We moved to Cambridge and our daughter went to school there. I spent my days writing. I started writing *The Game.* This was 1979/'80, and there wasn't the Internet, there wasn't e-mail, there wasn't FaceTime. There were letters, and letters would take three weeks for me to send, a couple of weeks for people to read and respond to, and another three weeks to get back to me. By that time, most of two months was gone and I wasn't as productive as I'd hoped to be.

I finished my book and the book tour. I was approached by the Davis government, in Ontario. They wanted to create a special office that would focus on youth unemployment and they would call the person the "Youth Commissioner of Ontario." Larry Grossman was the Treasurer of Ontario. He asked me if I was interested in the commissioner position. I said I was and started as Youth Commissioner in Ontario in 1984. It was a two-year appointment and ended almost three years later in late 1986.

During that time, I started talking to people about a different project. There had been some people at CBC who were interested in taking *The Game* and turning it into a TV series. I didn't know how it translated into a TV series, but it got me thinking. I wasn't interested in transforming *The Game* into a TV series but I thought there was a TV series that could be developed. Eventually, after writing *Home Game: Hockey and Life in Canada,* in 1990, CBC developed the book into a six-part documentary series.

I was turning 50. I had a friend who was on the Board of Directors of the Toronto Maple Leafs. They asked me if I was interested in becoming the President. I was hired to be the President of the Toronto Maple Leafs in 1997. That was the next part of my career. In 2004, I resigned from the Maple Leafs and went into Federal politics.

I was a Federal Liberal member of parliament from 2004 to 2011. We had four elections during that time. We were the government for the first 18 months. I was Minister of Social Development during this period. We were brought down in December of 2005. The election was at the end of January 2006, when we became Opposition until 2011, when I lost that election and left politics.

I love to read. I enjoy books, theatre, and travel. My wife and I love wandering around, driving, and taking secondary roads, whether it's renting a car in the U.S. Midwest, or elsewhere.

My Advice

- Ask yourself: "What's the most useful thing to do; what's the most interesting thing to do," then do it.

Name: Lorne B.
Occupation: Accountant
Retirement Age: 61
Current Age: 83
Protirement Activities: **New Career/Job;** Family Enthusiast

My Protirement Story

I have been retired for at least twenty years. I'm 83. The first year of retirement was totally taken up with the care of my wife and planning for my daughter's wedding. My wife was an RN and was determined to see her daughter married. She didn't live long after that. I maintained the house for another seven years.

I ended up selling my house and moving to a condo in St. Catharines. I dropped in on an old neighbour for a drink and he asked me what I was doing. I said, "Nothing; I'm bored." He said, "Oh, that's interesting." A couple of weeks later, he asked me to come on board and manage his family foundation. That was over twenty years ago, and I am still doing it. It gives me a chance to stay close to the market. I've got eight million dollars to invest, I give away about three and a half percent of their assets annually, and sometimes more. It keeps me involved. I have free time.

I work through the family members. We've got two committees, one Investment Committee and one is the Donations Committee. I've got a two-year-old grandson, with my 50 year-old son. I've got two granddaughters. One of them is now at Queen's University in nursing.

My Advice

- During the first year of retirement, say "no" to everything.
- Stay busy and active.
- If you are going to have a job, make sure it is flexible so you can travel and do other things.
- Take care of your health.

Name: Ray M.
Occupation: Accountant
Retirement Age: 60
Current Age: 81
Protirement Activities: **New Career/Job;** Seniorpreneur; Travel Enthusiast; Community Builder

My Protirement Story

In 1995, I retired, became the Director of Hockey Operations for the Owen Sound Attack, and ran the OHL hockey team. In

2000, we sold the team. I stayed and helped the new management. I've been here ever since. I am the business manager. I love talking to the hockey people. At 81, though, I think maybe I'll pack it in, sometime in the next six months or so.

In 1992, they put me in the local Sports Hall of Fame. It was a great honor.

My wife and I still do a lot of things. We travel in the summer, we've been on a few cruises, and other trips. I'm a director of our condo; I have looked after the trustees' money for our church for six years or seven years. I was also the Chair of the Police Board, and for the last ten years, I've been on the city's Finance Committee.

I know different people say to me, "Why don't you pack it in? Why don't you quit?" And it's a good question, but I think, as long as you're healthy and as long as you enjoy it, why change? I've a lot of interests. I don't know what it'd be like to get up four or five days in a row and not have anything to do, or not have any plans to go somewhere.

A lot of my friends, I can't believe the number of people, maybe it's because everybody is living longer, but a number of them have gotten Alzheimer's. I've read, or heard, that if you keep your mind active, and you keep busy, the chances are lessened. I don't know whether that's true or not, but...I believe that being idle is dangerous, there must be something to that.

My Advice

- Keep your mind active.
- Keep busy.
- If you enjoy your job, stay with it.
- Do something you enjoy.

Name:	Rabbi Steve G.
Occupation:	Rabbi & Educator
Retirement Age:	65
Current Age:	69
Protirement Activities:	**New Career/Job;** Hobbyist

My Protirement Story

In the summer of 2014, when I was 65, I retired. I knew that I could financially retire. I did some thinking about what I did and did not want to do. I did it in blocks of time. I divided my initial retirement into two-year blocks. In the first two years, I didn't want to do retired people things. I didn't want to play bridge five days a week, go to retired people luncheons, volunteer to be on the library board, etc.

In the first two years, I wanted to do everything I could to continue with the things that I really liked about my job, without having the obligations of doing them, and without having the time constraints. I would continue to do the things I really loved to do. That meant teaching, and bringing back an adult Jewish program through the Jewish Community Centre. There was a niche for someone to do inter-faith teaching. Social justice led me to continue to be active in inter-faith activities with Muslims and other communities. It led to doing a radio show on a Christian radio station.

Some of the challenges at the beginning of retiring, included going from having a very busy schedule to having no schedule. When I was working full time, people knew that I was in the gym by 8 o'clock and at work by 10 o'clock. Now people say, "You were not at the gym today?" I say, "I just came at a different time, some days I come at 6 o'clock and some days at 11 o'clock." I think that's the hardest thing, you don't have set schedule so you set your own schedule.

Certainly, the second hardest thing has been finding how I want to interact with people. When you retire, you're not required to meet with anybody and some people like to sit at home for 10 hours. They can read, they can have projects in the house. I haven't chosen to do that. I have a schedule now for when I go to the gym and for when I teach. The first year, I definitely made a schedule for the golf season. I knew when I played golf I'd interact with people. I knew when I taught I'd interact with people. I knew when I went to the gym I'd interact with people, and that made it less worrisome about the lack of personal interaction, which was important.

I probably have more breakfasts and lunches than I ever did before. Breakfast is with people who are still working and lunches are with people who aren't.

I decided that I wouldn't do any organized trips to Israel in the first two years, partly to allow the new leadership to decide what they would do in relation to trips. I have planned to lead a trip to Morocco and Spain next fall. That will be more community oriented and won't compete with any trips to Israel by the new Rabbi. I did my own personal travel to Israel and Florida this past winter, while my wife enjoyed the winter staying here and skiing.

The second two-year plan is predicated on whether the adult Jewish learning program I was working on got off the ground. It looks that way, so in the second two years, the idea is to continue with that and to find a meaningful volunteer activity that's not within the Jewish community.

Now that I have a better sense of my financial situation, travelling has more appeal. Taking cooking courses is still on my list, as well. I have wanted to do that for a while now.

My Advice

- In spite of what you do for work, it is important to develop one interest or activity separate from your vocation.
- Find a way to actualize it during your working career.

CHAPTER 8: PROTIREMENT CATEGORY #4: SENIORPRENEURS

"I Create.
I Take Risks.
I Live My Passion.
I am a SENIORPRENEUR!"
Ellis Katsof

Introduction

When I began the interviews, I expected that protirement activities would include volunteer work, hobbies, sports, travel, and other leisure related activities in addition to part-time and full-time employment. I did not expect to find many people embracing entrepreneurial business start-ups. I was surprised to find the entrepreneurial spirit is alive and well among older adults, and I have named this group, 'Seniorpreneurs'.

Boomers, between the ages of 50 and 65, make up the largest group of new entrepreneurs in the world.

Facts about "Seniorpreneurs"

The research is enlightening. Older adults, age 50 and above, are the fastest growing age group embracing business start-ups throughout the developed world. A 2012 CIBC report, *Start-ups — Present and Future*, by Benjamin Tal, identified that: "...the fastest growing segment of the start-up market is the 50 and over age group. This group now accounts for close to 30% of total start-ups, more than double the rate seen in the 1990s."[15]

Tal states that: "This trend represents not only an ageing North American society, but also an increased propensity to start a business among Baby Boomers. The affordability and availability of technology enable older North Americans to provide services from home. They are also able to use their well-developed skills and take advantage of their wide business networks and connections more effectively."

In a 2014 review of the literature related to the 'Grey Entrepreneur', Weber and Schaper identified that 31% of all Australian business start-ups were owned and operated by people over 50 years old.[16] In 2015, the US entrepreneurship think tank, The Kauffman Foundation, stated that entrepreneurship was highest among 55 to 64-year-olds. They found that 25.8% of individuals launching businesses in 2015 were between 55 and 64 years old, up from 14.8% in 1996.[17]

Seniors are launching businesses for many different reasons. Some want to keep working because they see it as a key to healthy living, keeping busy, and staying challenged. They want to follow their passion, be in control of their work environment, and feel good about themselves. Others have always wanted to own their own business and see this as an opportunity to fulfil this life-long goal. Some see it as a means to supplement their retirement income. Others are not ready to retire but feel it is their best chance of overcoming age discrimination and finding meaningful employment.

A 2013 AARP Report, *Staying Ahead of the Curve*, identified that seven in ten older adults planned to work during retirement. The main reasons for continuing to work included:

- 31% for enjoyment;
- 30% for the additional income;
- 21% for something interesting to do;
- 14% to stay physically active; and
- 11% to stay mentally active.

The Term "Seniorpreneur"

Why have I chosen the term Seniorpreneur to describe this group of entrepreneurs? Many different descriptors for this group have been used over the past 10 years, including Grey Entrepreneurs, Older Entrepreneurs, Senior Entrepreneurs, Boomerpreneurs, Zoomerpreneurs, and Seniorpreneurs. In 2006, Joe Wasylyk launched a Canadian project to address this new breed of entrepreneur. It was called, the 'Seniorpreneur Project'. In 2014, Wasylyk published, *Encore! Encore! Seniors (50+) as Entrepreneurs: Their Time has Come*. In his book, Wasylyk writes about a business model, Seniorpreneurship, which could: "help seniors regain control of hard-earned financial resources, and live the dream of an active, creative, and prosperous retirement life."[18]

The word 'Seniorpreneur' is now widely used in Australia to describe this phenomenon. There was little use of the word until 2012, when Australians began embracing the term. In March 2016, Dr. Ruth Williams wrote an article, *Seniorpreneurs - We Need You,* for the University of Melbourne. It discussed the importance of the Seniorpreneur in Australia. She stated that: "The emergence of the older entrepreneur, now commonly known as the 'Seniorpreneur', is proving to be the fastest growing segment of new business owners in Australia. Almost 35% of all new businesses are Seniorpreneur start-ups.[19] The average age of the Seniorpreneur was 57." The term 'Seniorpreneur' is beginning to be used in Canada, mostly in British Columbia.

Research has shown that the 50 to 65 age group is the largest age cohort becoming Seniorpreneurs in Canada, USA, Australia, UK, and Japan. I have chosen to use the term 'Seniorpreneur' because the term 'Seniorpreneur' aptly describes this group of energetic, creative, risk-taking individuals.

Why are Seniorpreneurs so successful?

The Seniorpreneur has many advantages over younger age groups when it comes to successfully launching new businesses. The literature from Canada, USA, and Australia all identify the same characteristics that help Seniorpreneurs be successful, including:

Well-established Networks

After a lifetime of working, Seniorpreneurs have developed extensive networks, far greater than Millennials who make up the second largest age group involved in new business start-ups. These networks provide Seniorpreneurs with easy access to consultants, advisors, mentors, investors, and consumers. Younger entrepreneurs are at a distinct disadvantage in regards to the breadth of their own personal networks that can be supportive of new business start-ups.

Experience

The Seniorpreneur has had extensive life and work experience they gained throughout their career. They often have experience in the many aspects of operating a business, such as: business planning, financial planning, marketing, human resources, purchasing, etc., and bring these skills, expertise, and knowledge to their start-up initiative. Boomers, because of their age, have also experienced successes and failures, and through this life experience, tend to have greater resiliency to bounce back when things do not work out as intended.

Skills and Knowledge

As a result of a lifetime of working, the Seniorpreneur has had the time and opportunity to develop a wide range of skills, as well as a deep knowledge base that can be leveraged when developing a new business.

Time to Devote to a Business Start-up

When we are younger, with family responsibilities, mortgages, and careers, it is difficult to carve out the time to dedicate to building a new business. Seniorpreneurs do not have the same obligations as a younger person, and usually have more time and flexibility to devote to starting up a new business than younger adults.

Financial Resources

The Seniorpreneur usually has more accumulated wealth and financial assets than the Millennial. The Seniorpreneur can use these financial assets to leverage support for a business start-up. This often allows the Seniorpreneur to take more risks and invest in a business opportunity more easily than when they were younger and had young families, mortgages, and greater financial liabilities.

"Seniorpreneur" Interests

The Seniorpreneurs I interviewed were involved in a wide variety of entrepreneurial activities. Many of them launched small businesses.

These Seniorpreneurs are also involved in a variety of other Protirement activities, including: Caregivers, Hobbyists, Travel Enthusiasts, Community Builders, Health Enthusiasts, and Life Long Learners.

"Seniorpreneur" Protirement Stories

I interviewed eleven individuals who were "Seniorpreneurs" in their Protirement. They range in age from 62 to 83. In the following stories, you will meet an amazing group of people who believe in the entrepreneurial, or Seniorpreneurial, spirit and who have kept it alive during their Protirement. The excitement and enthusiasm they have for their business ventures was infectious. Please join me in learning more about these individuals by reading their stories on the following pages.

"Seniorpreneur" personal Protirement Stories follow.

Name:	Andy Z.
Occupation:	Maintenance Mechanic, Plant Superintendent
Retirement Age:	60
Current Age:	68
Protirement Activities:	**Seniorpreneur,** Travel Enthusiast

My Protirement Story

Within the first week of retirement I was offered three full time jobs. One of them was at a car dealership. I walked in and asked the manager if they needed a driver. He asked me how much money I was asking for and I responded "I won't take a penny less than minimum wage." He seemed refreshed by this attitude, so I worked with him for a few months. At one point, my wife and I, and two of our teenagers were driving for them while we kicked around ideas for a craft business that we were conceptualizing.

About six months before I accepted the package for retirement, we dipped our toes into this rock candle business. My official retirement date was December 28th, and a month before that, we ventured into our first craft show in Stratford. It was a success. We almost sold out at that first show. We met other crafters at the shows and realized they were an amazingly close fraternity of unique, incredibly talented yet at the same time like-minded artists. We found the whole experience exhilarating, Meeting new friends at the craft shows was fun. The one-on-one interaction with customers has been infinitely satisfying.. It's a complete turnaround from what I did at my previous career. Instead of working in a manufacturing environment, I deal now with people on a much more social level. My wife and I engage in 30 to 35 shows a year, across Ontario, Manitoba, and Alberta.

I like to tell people, "It's never hard getting up at five in the morning when you don't have to." It's not unusual for me to make a dozen rock candles before breakfast. I worked shift work all my life and, in retirement, it's early to bed and early to rise.

We take a sabbatical in January, February, and March, and generally go to warmer climes for those months. The last couple of years, we have also reduced the workload in August and September. We have an RV, which we decided we don't use enough, and have gone to Hilton Head, Vermont, and the east coast of Canada among other local trips. When we travel, it's pleasure, but we take the opportunity to explore quarries for rock for the candles.

I am 68 now. I will probably wind down the candle business when I am 70. This year we decided we would cut back on summer shows and do more for ourselves. It's not the money that is driving us in the candle business. We do it to meet people, stay busy, and just have something to do. It's not healthy just sitting around after you retire. I remember my father saying "The best years of your life are when you retire and you still have your health." I totally believe that and I still have way too much energy to just stop.

Advice

- Whatever you do, have fun.
- Take what life gives you and enjoy it.
- Find something that gives you a purpose.

Name:	Brian U.
Occupation:	Psychologist; Management Consultant
Retirement Age:	58
Current Age:	70
Protirement Activities:	**Seniorpreneur;** Community Builder

My Protirement Story

In 2004, at the age of 58, I retired from my management consulting business and got back together with an old friend who was running the Canadian arm of a company called, Executive Committee. We started working on building the company, but a month before the launch, my partner was nearly killed in a car accident. That got us thinking about what we wanted to be doing. We were living on a farm in Caledon at the time and had converted the barn into a seasonal art gallery.

We saw the need for creating a magazine or a media vehicle, which we called, *Arabella*, with the view of supporting and promoting Canadian artists or creative organisations to the widest possible audience.

Our magazine, *Arabella*, is trying to help aspiring, achieving, and accomplished artists. We chose to look at the magazine world and do everything that they didn't do. For us, creativity was, "let's not follow the pack, let's do something different." What keeps us alive is the sense that we are always trying to do something different.

We are aware of those age markers. We had the opportunity of applying for CPP, but as a state of mind, NO! I never had a sense of retiring. There were consultants who would count the days to retirement. That was really demoralising for me, in that I realised I didn't want to live my life that way. I couldn't see myself sitting there until some mythical thing called, 'retirement', happened.

When I was with the school board, I researched the career patterns and successes of principals, and it was alarming the number of high school principals who were dead within two years of retirement. Upon retirement, they lost everything, their sense of authority, and contact with people.

We live in St. Andrews, New Brunswick, a small community where I have gotten involved in some volunteer activities. There is an island here that William Van Horne, who finished the Canadian Railway for CP, built a summer estate. The estate has both provincial and federal heritage designations and we are fundraising to preserve the estate, given its historic significance.

My Advice

- Take the activities you really feel interested in and pursue them.
- Nurture your interests, shift around your activities, and be flexible.
- Continue looking for the things you are interested in, and see where they take you.
- If money is important, figure which activities will give you the money.
- Listen to other people, don't fight them, they can give you valuable insight, but then make your own decisions.

Name: Gil Amelio
Occupation: CEO, Tech Firms
Retirement Age: 56
Current Age: 74
Protirement Activities: **Seniorpreneur**, Community Builder; Family Enthusiast

My Protirement Story

I was 65 when I left the corporate world and hung out my shingle. The number one reason for hanging out my shingle was that I really enjoyed what I did; I loved the industry, and really enjoyed mentoring young people. Consulting and mentoring younger people keeps me engaged and doing things. I find that when I am active it keeps me younger. Most people who look at me never guess my age and think I am much younger.

I think, if it is done in the right way, it is a great way to stay in contact with the world that you were a part of, while still having your own life. This is more enjoyable, from a family point of view, but I am also getting to meet a lot of interesting people.

It was a downer when I initially left the corporate world. I was concerned that maybe I wasn't useful, maybe I had gotten to be old and crotchety, and maybe no one "loved me" anymore. I think that's a common experience. As a consequence, it's a bit of a downer. I think I handled it well, but some mornings I would wake up and think, "What am I going to do today?" Having had this lifestyle of working 10 or 12 hours a day, year after year, you suddenly have this incredible vacuum when you stop working. There is a void to be filled.

One of the first things I did, before fully retiring, was to get involved in charity work to give me something to do. I joined the Board of the American Film Institute, a not-for-profit institute, and stayed there until 2013.

When I retired in 2008, I didn't have much to do other than charity work. Between 2008 and 2010, I couldn't find the kind of projects where I thought I could make significant contributions. During this lull, I wasn't a happy guy although I kept a smile on my face. I used to know what I was going to do every day, and it was a very awkward feeling to suddenly have no schedule and no focus, but I finally got through that.

Pretty soon, I had more invitations than I had the ability to handle. So, I decided to limit my engagements to a maximum of five simultaneous clients.

I would advise anybody, who has been active in business and really loved the industry that they were a part of, to stay connected and to continue to participate; but they should participate in a very different way, as an advisor and thought stimulator. I honestly think that people over 65 years old can contribute enormous amounts to the development of companies. They possess great life experience and a certain accumulated wisdom. I find the younger group, as smart as they are, have not yet attained what I call 'wisdom'. What I do is provide that 'wisdom', and I can't tell you how fulfilling it is.

In 2018, I turn 75, and my wife would like me to begin phasing out of my consulting activity to spend more time with the family. One of my granddaughters is now at the University of Nevada, about 20 miles from where we live now. Our children are starting to get gray hair and our grandchildren are getting to be adults. I think my wife is probably right. I am getting ready to transition to the next stage, which will be much more family focused, in order to leave a legacy when we are gone.

But right now, I am not ready for that, I still have work to do! I have three companies that are on the cusp of going big time and it is very exciting. I think, within the next three years, all three companies will come of age, and what a great memory to have—I was there, mentoring these guys, and now they are successful businesses.

My Advice

- Plan for your retirement like you plan for everything else.
- Start planning years before you retire.
- Maintain your relationships and work friendships after you retire.
- Continue to be available.
- Stay engaged.

Name:	Jacquie H-W.
Occupation:	EAP Business Owner, Consultant
Retirement Age:	NA
Current Age:	NA
Protirement Activities:	**Seniorpreneur**; Community Builder

My Protirement Story

In 2005, I merged my company with what is now Morneau Shepell and stayed on as a consultant. I went from Jacquie Herman Associates to Jacquie Herman Consulting.

I have never planned retirement. Although I have the option to retire I don't see retirement happening. I always loved what I was doing, I loved raising my children, I loved working in the CWL, I loved working in the leadership roles, I got absolutely excited seeing people grow. It was a repeat of the same pattern. If a door opens I go through it and explore a new opportunity.

So, where I am now is a dilemma because I basically spooked myself for whatever reason by getting business cards printed, which I am going to have absolutely no need for. I continue to do work for Morneau Shepell because they give me the opportunity to do what I like best, work with people. I don't like administration and most of it is done for me.

My Advice

- Do what is your passion.
- Whatever you do, do it well.
- Never fear change.

Name: Jimmy P.
Occupation: Radio Jingle Producer; Corporate Event Producer
Retirement Age: 64
Current Age: 74
Protirement Activities: **Seniorpreneur**

My Protirement Story

At the age of 64, after 40 years of selling radio jingles and corporate entertainment, I left the corporate event world and started up an entertainment company called, 'Curtain Call Entertainment'. Now, I put tours together for my various shows, which can be exciting, but is also a risk that can run over $250,000. Renting the theatre alone can cost you up to $13,000 a night, never mind another $10,000 for marketing *plus* the cost of wages, accommodations, travel, and food for up to 18 people. It's a big bill and a risky business, but I am very proud of my Grand Old Opry show, which I've titled: "Welcome to Nashville." I am also doing an Abba show titled: "The ABBA Story."

I book the shows across Canada, in theatres of 1,000 seats or more; theatres like Kitchener's beautiful 2000-seat Centre in The Square, and Stratford's amazing 1100-seat Avon Theatre.

Had I played my cards right when I was younger, I probably wouldn't be working as much as I do now, but when you love the business as much as I do, who wants to retire anyway?

My Advice

- Don't sweat the small stuff.

Name: John KW.
Occupation: Investment Manager
Retirement Age: 58
Current Age: 60
Protirement Activities: **Seniorpreneur**

My Protirement Story

I retired as an investment manager at the age of 58. I had a month of just mucking around doing nothing. Most of my friendships were work related and my work life was very office oriented. Suddenly, when I retired, I had nowhere to go in the morning. Since my social life at work was very much a part of my day, there was a sudden drop off in my social life. I quickly found that all of my social networks at work disintegrated.

My brother, who had left the banking world about 10 years earlier, had started up his own corporate finance group and was out raising money for companies. We had discussed doing something together, so we initially started working together in July of 2014 on a few deals that he had brought to the table.

We saw some opportunities for a venture targeted at the medical marijuana market, not on the grow side, but taking a process for the extract from cannabis products and taking the non-hallucinogenic extract out of the marijuana and putting it into a time released tablet, making it as close to a pharma product as you can.

Another thing that I did when I retired was to keep some routines. For instance, my wife and I always walked or drove to work together. Once I retired, I decided to get up at the same time and continue to drive my wife to work. Most days I also pick her up. That routine has been very helpful for both of us.

When I retired, I applied for the Director Program at the Rotman Business School, received my ICD.D certification, and am looking for opportunities to join boards in either the corporate world or the non-profit world.

My Advice

- You can't start planning for your retirement years too early. It really creeps up on you fast.
- You can try to plan, but I think most things just happen to you as time goes on.
- It is important to have a hobby while you are working that you can continue when you retire. You can then build on that hobby and do new things, as well.

- You should get involved with organizations before you retire, if you know that you want to be involved with them after retirement.
- Extend your social life beyond work friends.
- Exercise and stay active.

Name:	John Dan J.
Occupation:	Coal Miner
Retirement Age:	65
Current Age:	83
Protirement Activities:	**Seniorpreneur;** Family Enthusiast

My Protirement Story

(John Dan's daughter, Gale, joined in the interview so the story is told by both John Dan and his daughter Gale.)

We opened this place (Seagull Restaurant) in 1975 and I was still working in the mines. I stopped working in the mines around 1992.

(Gale) My dad still works in the restaurant. That keeps him young, keeps him going. He comes in early. He was here when we got here at 7:30 this morning. He already had the turkey in the oven, and he had just made his chowder. He also makes the coconut cream pies. Then, at night, he and I are the last two to leave here. It can be between 10:00 and 10:30 p.m. We close at 8:00 p.m. and then clean up. He's back down here early in the morning. He'll go home for a little rest in the afternoon, but that's it.

Yes, it keeps him young, keeps him going. That's what he says. When we tell him to go home to Sydney Mines, he says, "Well, what would I do? At least I know, when I get up in the morning, what I'm going to do while I'm here; but if I was home, I'd get up in the morning and say, 'What am I going to do this morning?'" He knows what's ahead of him every morning here. He moves back down here in May, and stays 'til the end of October. Then he goes to Florida in April and May. As soon as he gets home from

Florida, he's two days in Sydney Mines and then moves down here and we start getting the restaurant ready.

In the fall, when we close, him and I, we clean all the deep-fryers; clean all the range hoods; clean everything. He disconnects the water, and does all the plumbing. We shut everything down; the power gets shut off, so we have to make sure the lines are cleared. He does all that.

He's 83 and he's going to get his passport renewed with a 10-year passport. He would say, "Just keep going." Dad doesn't believe in sitting in the chair and staying in the house, even when he's home in Sydney Mines. He walks with his friend, a lady friend. They walk every morning. And then they go to Tim Horton's for a cup of coffee. He snow blows his yard. He's got an upstairs in his house, where his bedroom is, so he has to be going up and down the stairs all the time. He says that's what keeps him healthy. He always says, "If you sit in the chair and don't move, Alzheimer's will set in, but if you keep your body going, your mind keeps going."

My Advice

- Just keep going.
- Don't sit in the chair all day.
- Don't stay in the house all day.
- Stay busy.

Name: Karel Z.
Occupation: Tinsmith
Retirement Age: 50
Current Age: 57
Protirement Activities: **Seniorpreneur;** Caregiver; Health Enthusiast; Family Enthusiast

My Protirement Story

I retired from General Motors when I was 50. My wife and I had been running Willow Den, a gift store, for four years by the time I could retire. I was responsible for doing the books and helping her with ordering and during the week I would come in after my shift at the plant to spell her for the last three hours of the day.

The year before I could retire, the company offered me an inverse seniority, optional layoff. It was a real bonus because it was like a phased-in retirement. I had that first year to get through the heebie-jeebies, and say, "Oh my gosh, I'm not going to be making 'blah' per hour anymore, and I don't have the option of overtime every few weeks; can we make it on one-third of our salary?"

There was no major transition, except I stopped punching a clock for somebody else and started being wholly dedicated to our business, seven days a week when necessary.

Initially I felt like an interloper in my wife's world because she was used to seeing me gone at 6:00 am and now I was hanging around until 9:00, 9:30, and then jumping in the car with her and going to *her* place of work. There was a bit of a transition and learning experience for both of us that way. We were learning to share, and learning that we each needed space, and learning not to take things personally just because she'd need space, or I needed space.

When I'm outside of the store, life is, for the most part, focused on spirit work. We start our days early; we're usually on the streets by 5:30 in the morning, walking. I love to go for an early-morning walk. We live on a ravine on the Twelve-Mile Creek so we can start our day in nature; with quiet time in the backyard; just kind of starting our day together, working through anything that we need to look at. Business discussions sometimes happen there or just discussions about where we are, and what our dreams and next steps are going to be. Part of my life involves yoga; I'm a certified yoga teacher who does not teach.

Spending time with our grandkids is special. We have two living down the street from us; my daughter is seven doors down from us and two who live in the far north. School for the two grandchildren down the street is right around the corner from us so on Monday, Grandma picks up the boys after school, and on Thursday its Grandpa's turn because Grandpa has yoga class in the evening. We want to be able to see the two northern boys for longer periods of time but for now, our business is a growing concern and it keeps visits too short.

My wife and I are not relying on others to support us until the day we die; pension funds can change, government programs are limited. We have invested in ourselves doing something we both love. In an earlier time there were old farmers in the fields, European farmers, who would continue to work until the day they couldn't get up because they were committed to and found worth in what they did. I want to be doing as much as I can with the time and energy that I have, because our time here is short.

My Advice

- Whatever you do in life, do it without fear.
- In all life decisions trust your heart and trust that if you do everything that's set in front of you to the best of your ability, you will be successful.
- Rely on nobody else to support you in your needs. Rely on people to help you, but in the end, rely on yourself for your own happiness.

Name:	Mario C.
Occupation:	Teacher, Vice-Principal, Principal, Superintendent
Retirement Age:	55
Current Age:	58
Protirement Activities:	**Seniorpreneur;** Health Enthusiast

My Protirement Story

I retired as a superintendent of education from the Niagara Catholic District School Board when I was 55. I purchased a gourmet burger franchise and opened 'The Works' in St Catharines. I have dealt with servicing students, parents and staff all my life so customer service was part of who I was. People are often curious about how I went from education to the restaurant business. Business was in my family since I was 10. My family ran an Italian food store in Niagara Falls called Franks Food Market for over 12 years. My childhood is full of memories of the experiences from that store. In my post secondary years I went back and worked in the store during the summer months.

I saw how hard my parents worked; I saw the lows and highs of business. I saw what they did, I saw the sacrifices, but I also saw what a family run business could do for you. I loved the buzz of being in business...the social part of it and, of course, the successes. I realized early, that business was in my blood.

Early in my education career, I often questioned if I had made the right decision. Eventually, after six or seven years in education, I felt comfortable that I made the right decision. My career, having been surrounded by students and colleagues, whom I'm still friends with, has been a very worthwhile and memorable one.

My everyday friends and social circle were not part of my educational sector. So, upon retirement, I had those friends to turn to and socialize with. I still get together with my educational friends, as well, but most of them work and with time you tend to drift toward your high school friends and neighbors...at least I did.

I had virtually no transition from education to owning and running a restaurant. My daughter was managing alongside of me, and if there was a transition, it was my relationship with my daughter. We had to get to know each other in a different setting on a different level. We didn't always see eye to eye, but we learned to listen to each other, and once we did it worked out well. My wife is also involved in the business, in charge of finances, which is so important to any business.

I have more free time now than when I was an educator. I do more things around the house and am able to spend more time with my mom and my family. If I want to go into work at nine in the morning I do. If I want to go in at two in the afternoon, I go in at two. The nice thing is that I am not on a schedule or watching the clock. I have no evening meetings or reports to prepare and present. I can take vacations at different times of the year, instead of only at March break or in the summer, which are normally peak times.

I am now on a workout regiment where I spend three to four times a week in a gym. I was never able to do that during my career. I can meet with my friends during the day for coffee, or lunch.

I have friends who retired but were then hired back as consultants in the same company and are working harder than they were before

I also have friends who retired, and then went through a down period that led to depression, because they had nothing to do once they retired. They had never thought about the effects of retirement and all of a sudden there was this huge void. I don't have that void. I am retired, but I guess I am not. Maybe I am semi-retired. I filled the void doing something I want to be doing. I'll know when the time comes to retire for good—my body will tell me, my mind will tell me. I'm not there, and I hope I'm not there for a long time.

I have no problem going for another five or ten years, as long as I have my health. If I give this up one day, is there something else around the corner? If God continues to bless me with good health we'll see.... I am having too much fun to consider making plans for my retirement.

My Advice

- Have fun with whatever you decide to do, even if that means not retiring.
- Do your own thing, be your own boss.
- Position yourself so that you can call the shots and decide on what is right for you....listen to your gut not the noise.
- Keep busy.
- Fill your days with what you want to do. Some people may call it work, but as long as you can call it play, it's never work.
- Never judge someone else's decision on retiring or not retiring...you're not them.

Name:	Terry O'Reilly
Occupation:	Co-founder of Pirate Radio & Television, a creative audio production company
Retirement Age:	53
Current Age:	57
Protirement Activities:	**Seniorpreneur**; Community Builder; Writer/Performer; Family Enthusiast

My Protirement Story

I worried about losing my power base in the advertising business when I sold my interests in my radio and television production company at the age of 53. I worried because a power base is important. I could pick up the phone and call a creative director and get a favor. But it was an unnecessary worry. It's been almost five years now, but it really hasn't diminished. I think the radio show is a great part of that, because the industry listens to the show and knows I'm still immersed in the business. When I pick up the phone to call, they're still as responsive as they ever were, so that worry, really, was unfounded.

I was really fortunate. I think a lot of people worry about what they are going to do after they retire. People would say to me, "What are you going to do when you leave Pirate?" I said, "I'll have lots of things to do." They would say, "I couldn't retire; I would just be bored." I would say, "Yeah, I get that, I'm only leaving the running of a company, I'm not 'retiring.' I'm 'protiring.'

The radio show is a big part of my third chapter. I don't even know how I managed to produce it while I was running Pirate at the same time. When I look back, I don't know how I juggled all those balls. It's a seven-day-a-week proposition to do a weekly radio show with the small team I have. But leaving Pirate gave me more time, so now I'm not working day *and* night. I'm working full days and I actually have time with my wife at night.

One of the wonderful things about leaving Pirate was that we got to spend every day together and have dinner together every night. That was a huge thing for me because I'm a big family guy. Seeing more of my daughters was a wonderful benefit, too.

My original plan was to work half the week and then have half the week to myself, where I could start plowing through the books stacked beside my bed. That went right out the window. With the exception of July and August, I work seven days a week, every week, to produce the show. I also have a very busy speaking career. Delivering keynote talks at marketing conferences takes me across the country, so I'm travelling a lot.

I'll do between 20 and 30 keynote talks a year, in almost as many cities. I also do very selective consulting. I only pick opportunities that are really interesting to me, or where I think I can really make a difference, and I say no to everybody else. But between those three things, it's seven days a week. This past year, I wrote a book that came out in February. So, last summer's time off was taken up with writing the book, and last fall was filled with editing the book. I really haven't had much of a break in the last two years. But it's all good.

That's the big difference. I'm only doing what I want to do, now. I loved co-founding and growing Pirate, but now that the weight of running a company is off my shoulders—or off my heart—it is a wonderful thing. That's the joy of this chapter of my life.

My wife, Debbie, runs our business, which is comprised of the radio show, consulting, book marketing, and speaking. She's the Executive Producer of the radio show, which is a huge undertaking. It's a weekly national radio show and is also on Sirius satellite, which requires a different version of the show. I'm also on WBEZ in Chicago, which involves another version of the show. Then there is the podcast, which involves yet another version of the show. We do promos every week and we put out transcripts and visual elements people so can follow along. My wife has to run all of that, and it is a big, big machine, with lots of moving parts. She's also my speaking agent. She books me across the country, plus my travel, hotels, contracts, etc. She also does the same with my consulting. She is really the backbone, and we love working together.

You know, it's interesting, even if we're having a quick sandwich in the kitchen and talking business, it's still pretty wonderful. I love spending time with my wife. I love it. We've been married thirty-three years and I still love spending time with her.

My Advice

- Don't worry about what the next chapter is going to be. If you're passionate about what you do, there'll be an avenue that streams off your career, which will give you a wonderful 'Act III'.
- Look at your career from a 30,000-foot view and pluck out the things you love most. See if there's a way you can use those 'passion elements' when you transition into your third act.
- If you can't find anything to pluck out, then take a left at Albuquerque and head in a completely new direction. There's nothing wrong with that, either.

Name: Governor Tom Ridge
Occupation: Governor of Pennsylvania, Secretary of Homeland Security
Retirement Age: 60
Current Age: 71
Protirement Activities: **Seniorpreneur**; Hobbyist; Community Builder

My Protirement Story

My first year after concluding over twenty five years of public service provided multiple speaking opportunities. Thereafter I started a company now identified as "Ridge Global" after several iterations. Primarily my work is focused on disruptive technologies, risk management and cyber security. As a small business man I have the flexibility to be very selective about the subjects and the people with whom I work.

I have also had the opportunity to serve on several corporate boards and to devote time to non-profit causes I believe in. My primary non-profit interest is in the National Organization on Disability. I have been privileged to serve as the Chairman of the Board of Directors for over a decade. For too long we have ignored the reality that people with disabilities have talents that can and should be utilized by employers.

I'm not even sure it was a conscious decision to keep on working after I retired from public service. As long as I enjoy what I'm doing, and the people with whom I'm working, I'm going to keep working. It's just not in my DNA to retire.

At the end of the day, if I can say, "It was a productive day; I am happy I lived it", I am content. That happiness or self-satisfaction may be around family, around extracurricular activities, or around business interest. At our age we want to be productive, to contribute, and to make a difference.

My Advice

- At the end of every single day feel good about how you spent the preceding 12 or 14 hours.
- If you wake up in the morning and you're of good health and good mind then figure out a way to enjoy the balance of the day.

CHAPTER 9: PROTIREMENT CATEGORY #5: CAREGIVERS

"One person caring for another represents life's greatest value."
John Rohn

Introduction

Baby Boomers are often described as the "Sandwich Generation;" caring for their parents and children. As Boomers age, their caregiving roles are also extending to their grandchildren. I interviewed seven people who identified Caregiving as a primary Protirement activity. They were involved in caregiving relationships with their mothers and fathers, children, grandchildren, and close friends.

Facts about Caregivers

Today, Boomers are caregiving for multiple generations, including for their aging parents, ill spouses, children (both adult and young children), and for their grandchildren. According to Statistics Canada, in 2011, 12% of all caregivers in Canada were seniors.[20]

Due to advancements in health care and technology, seniors are living longer lives. As life expectancies increase, Boomers are finding themselves caring for aging parents in greater numbers. At the same time, millennial children are returning home, or not leaving as quickly, because it is taking them longer to establish themselves in careers. Cost of housing in larger urban centers is also a major factor for millennials remaining at home longer. In addition, Boomers find themselves caregiving for adult children who are ill or disabled and require ongoing support. Therefore, Boomers are finding themselves providing care for both their parents and adult children.

On the far end of this spectrum we find Boomers now caring for grandchildren. Sixty percent of Canadians between 55 and 64 years old are grandparents. This increases to 87% for those aged 65 to 74. With the cost of child care a challenge for many young families, Boomers are being called upon in greater numbers to provide care for their grandchildren.

There is also a small number of Boomer men who are finding themselves retired but suddenly starting new families, and spending significant amounts of their time caregiving for their own young children.

"Caregiver" Protirement Stories

I interviewed four Boomers who were involved in Caregiving as a major Protirement activity. They ranged in age from 59 to 72.

"Caregiver" personal Protirement Stories follow.

Name: Claire W.
Occupation: Non-Profit Executive
Retirement Age: 71
Current Age: 72
Protirement Activities: **Caregiver**; Community Builder; Health Enthusiast; Family Enthusiast

My Protirement Story

I knew there were going to be a lot of things to do when I retired because I was looking after my mother and spending time with my two grandsons. I have a large family and there are always lots of things going on with them. My mother was getting worse and worse, so it took up more and more of my time. I am also on a committee with the city. They are building a monument for people in the community, like Peter Kormos, who have excelled. I have been on the committee since it began, and I am helping with fund raising. I also go to the gym daily.

My Advice

- Make sure you have hobbies.
- Build your networks, keep up your relationships.
- Be open to continual learning.

Name: Donny L.
Occupation: Automotive Manufacture, Multiple jobs at General Motors
Retirement Age: 50
Current Age: 59
Protirement Activities: **Caregiver**; New Career/Job, Hobbyist

My Protirement Story

I retired in 2007. When I retired, it was two or three months before I realized I wasn't going back. I had to figure out what I was going to do as I was only 50 years old.

When I retired, the girls were in school all day and my wife was at work, so I started renovations at home and around the community. In 2009, I got a job at the Water Source and delivered water three days a week. I did that for about seven months. I liked the driving around, meeting different people, it was quite interesting. But, then, I had a snow mobile accident and fractured my thumb. That was the end of my water delivery career.

Once my thumb was healed, I went back to school and took some courses on how to drive a fork lift. My neighbour had a sheet metal business, doing flashings and copper work. He asked me to work at a hotel where he was doing some renovations and installing aluminum flashings and window casings. I did that from

October to June. It was interesting work and I learned a lot of stuff doing the job.

In the meantime, I renovated our cottage. My wife was still working and the kids were active in dance, jujitsu, singing, and piano. They were in and out the door seven days a week and needed one of us to deliver them everywhere. One of our daughters also started rowing, which meant the end of our summers up north. Last year, we bought a house in Florida and I renovated it.

In the meantime, my mother's health deteriorated over the years. The last four or five years, I was at her house five or six times a day for breakfast, lunch, and supper. She didn't drive, so I took her to all of her appointments with doctors and dentists, as well as shopping, etc. Thank God I got to hang out with my mother in that environment. You can never take that away from me. I loved it.

It's been a real void and I have to figure out what am I doing now, it's really huge. I have to figure out what's the next part of the journey. My daughter's are driving now, my wife's now retired. I am going to be 60 this year. So, I am not sure what is next.

My Advice

- Enjoy life.
- Be sure you are ready to step away from your career.
- Keep busy, step away gradually.
- Explore new things.
- It's a beginning of a new life, enjoy it.

Name: Sam C.
Occupation: Fire Fighter, Captain
Retirement Age: 60
Current Age: 64
Protirement Activities: **Caregiver;** Hobbyist; Community Builder

My Protirement Story

I come from a hard working family and have worked all my life. I came from Italy as a landed immigrant. I have worked one way or another since I was eight. So, when you ask me about retirement, retirement is very hard for someone who has worked all their lives. It's hard to just stop. It's like putting the brakes on.

It was hard leaving behind my friends, the job, the respect, the authority, and being important. I was looking after the city and now I am looking after vacuuming. It was a big change for me.

As a firefighter, you had to retire at age 60. I knew that was my last ride. The next day, I was looking for something; something was missing. After 42 years of always working, getting up, it didn't matter what I was doing, doing cement, moonlighting, I was getting up and I had a purpose. Now I get up but you can't keep busy 365 days a year. People say, "I am going to travel," but you can't travel a whole year. You can travel for a month but you have another 11 months.

As far as retirement, I am getting used to it now. I don't think I could go back to work. I miss the guys, I miss the friendships. They say retirement is the golden years but I don't feel that.

I look after my mother, and I have my wife to spend time with, but I don't plan my days. I don't get up and plan anything. I get up and if I decide I want to do something I do it, and if I don't feel like doing it, I don't do it. Everything is flexible for me. I bowl with some friends a couple of times week. I help out my mother and my sister, whose husband died a few years ago. If you are with your spouse all the time, you get on each other's nerves. If we are both around all the time, I get under her feet. That's a hard part.

I'll stay in bed until 10 o'clock, I'll watch TV, I don't care, and that's why I retired. To do what I want. You are the master of your destiny. In the summer, I bike ride and go for walks. We have a pool and I spend time taking care of the pool and enjoying it, and gardening. I still enjoy working in my computer shop downstairs. I also still do some handy work around the house and in the community.

Retirement is someone telling you, you are washed up, you are done. Retirement is strange, it is like you are really good until you get to this point, and then you are done! It is like the last chapter in your life. You know what comes after that and no one wants to get to there.

My Advice

- Find something that is important to you and do it.

Name:	Susan M.
Occupation:	Government Administrator
Retirement Age:	55
Current Age:	60
Protirement Activities:	**Caregiver**; Hobbyist

My Protirement Story

It was a strange time because I was busy right up until the time I retired. My daughter was moving home from university. Suddenly, both my kids were back home and we had a very full house. I felt like I was on vacation. After a few weeks, I started going for walks. My husband still had his routine and was doing his own thing. There is a mall near our house. I would walk there, get a coffee, and read. Some of my other friends were retired and we started meeting for coffee.

Retirement became like a long vacation. I missed my friends from work. I keep in touch with some of them. This is something that is interesting about retirement for me: my self-worth was never wrapped around work, so that's probably why I don't miss the actual work. I don't feel like I have lost any brainpower or anything just because I am no longer working; I feel the same, just less tired.

Because I was always running out the door fairly early, when I was working, I was never there to make breakfast for them; my husband was the morning parent. So now, I can get up and make breakfast for them as though I was a stay-at-home mom, even though they are now adults. I am not sure how I got the meals made, got the kids to soccer, answered the BlackBerry, when I was working.

About eight months into my retirement, my parent's health began to change. My 90-year-old father had minor prostate surgery that set him into a decline with infections. I was thrown immediately into the caregiver role, dealing with the Community Care Access Centre (CCAC). My mom was 87 and had Parkinson's, so she wasn't that great, either. We had nurses coming in, neurology appointments to go to, and I was coordinating all of it.

My mother was nervous about being at home at night with my father. Trying to get CCAC help was horrible. We eventually placed my dad into a nursing home that was in a different town from where my disabled sister was. I had to drive him to the home with my mother waving at the window. Then my mother needed to be placed in a home because she couldn't stay on her own. We also decided to put the house up for sale. I was managing all of that. It was the winter of 2013 and my disabled sister was in a home in Stayner, while my father was in a home in Collingwood.

It was a cold, wintry day when I got a call on my cell, in the middle of a snow storm, that they had a bed for my dad in the same nursing home in Stayner where my sister was living. Two hours later, they called me back to say there was another bed for my mother, but she also had to move in by Friday. It was now Wednesday. We were in shock. My poor mother, she suddenly had two days to change her life and move. Meanwhile, the house was up for sale. Thankfully, I don't know what I would have done if I wasn't retired. I don't know how I would have dealt with these challenges if I had been working.

My daughter moved home from university around May 2013, and started a program at George Brown College. My daughter is still playing soccer for George Brown College and for a women's league, so I am back to going to soccer games. I got to a game in time to see her score a goal and then fall and break her ankle. I had been at the hospital all day with my dad and then headed out to Sunnybrook Hospital with my daughter. I spent the next six weeks of that autumn as her chauffeur, because she couldn't drive and had just started school.

My sister died in February 2015. That was not a nice time but she had a long life, considering her disabilities. It was nice that my parents had a year together with her in the same home. My parents were going downhill, my father is quite frail, and he was a bit forgetful, but he still had his memory. My mother eventually passed away.

My Advice

- Allow yourself to just enjoy retirement.
- You don't have to do anything just because you feel guilty.
- Do something that makes you feel good.
- Do things if you want to—volunteer, work, hobbies.

CHAPTER 10: PROTIREMENT CATEGORY #6: POLITICAL ACTIVISTS

"Never doubt that a small group of thoughtful, committed citizens can change the world; indeed, it's the only thing that ever has."
Margaret Mead

Introduction

Civil rights, the sexual revolution, women's liberation, and Vietnam War protests were all an integral part of the Baby Boomer's growing up experience. Boomers became politically active at a young age. As Boomers retire, some are deciding to pursue those long lost political activist goals. For some, elected office becomes a goal, for others, supporting a political party as a volunteer becomes the goal.

Facts about Political Activists

It is unclear how many Boomers are involved in politics after retirement, but an analysis of Canada's current members of Parliament find that 28 members are between the ages of 65 and 69, while 12 members are between the ages of 70 and 75. According to a 2016 research study by the Rural Ontario Institute, 69% of Ontario Municipal Councillors were between the ages of

50 and 70.[21] It is unclear how many of them got involved in municipal politics after they retired from other careers, but it is clear that municipal politics is open to the older adult.

"Political Activists" Protirement Stories

I interviewed three Boomers who were Political Activists as primary Protirement activities. They ranged in age from 64 to 71. Two were elected officials at the municipal and regional government levels. The third was active in her Federal Riding Association. One of my interviewees who is "Not Retired" is also involved in politics, as a federal politician.

"Political Activist" personal Protirement Stories follow.

Name:	Carlos G.
Occupation:	Business Planning Consultant
Retirement Age:	67
Current Age:	71
Protirement Activities:	**Political Activist**; Caregiver; Travel Enthusiast; Community Builder

My Protirement Story

The last six or seven years, I hadn't done much because my wife had suffered from progressive arthritis and mobility issues and needed my help. Although I have been partially retired for many years, I finally fully retired from my business planning consulting about four years ago, in 2013. We started taking cruises, even though it wasn't my preferred way of travel, but it was easier for my wife. We came back from a cruise and a couple of months later, my wife began complaining of severe stomach pain. Her health got progressively worse. Caregiving became almost a full-time job. Sadly, I lost my wife of 43 years early in 2014, and it was an election year. Friends strongly encouraged me to run. I said if I was going to run I would run for a city position rather than a regional position. I did run for the city. I worked hard and I walked to all 7500 homes in Port Dalhousie Ward. I ended up getting elected with the third highest vote total.

I have been a City Councilor since 2014. I am a founding member of the Port Beautification and Works Committee (BWC). I am still very active with the Port Dalhousie Conservancy and other heritage organizations. I also try to support the arts in every way possible. I think I am working more now than when I was really working.

My Advice

- Plan what you will be doing.
- Need to keep your mind active with social intercourse, you need to keep inter-activity with other people.
- Keep busy with personal interests.
- Keep physically fit.

Name: Jane D.
Occupation: Psychology Professor
Retirement Age: 66
Current Age: 71
Protirement Activities: **Caregiver; Political Activist;** Hobbyist

My Protirement Story

In 2010, I retired from my position as a psychology professor at the University. When I first stopped working, there were days of anxiety. I was used to deadlines. Then, all of a sudden, it's gone. How should I best fill my time? All of a sudden, you feel your time is all flying through your fingers, sliding through…and you're not catching it, and it could be wasted!

One of the things you teach is that people should always have plans for when they retire. Well, I had no plans, other than enjoying the morning sun in my kitchen while reading the morning paper. But all kinds of things still needed to be done. It's like a panic you feel; "how should I structure this day?"

One of the things I did, when I knew I was going to retire, was order *The Globe and Mail* so I'd have it every morning. I thought the idea of having a coffee and reading the paper in the morning sounded awfully good, but I still felt like I was wasting time!

Yes, there are tensions, anxieties, and so on. And also, a feeling of…you know, there's mixed feelings. But then, that summer when I retired, we had been holding off on getting our house renovated, so that was my first job, organizing the renovations.

The next year, in spring, our youngest son got married, and the wedding was here, at this house, and so I took on the role of wedding planner. When I first retired, I could suddenly help my daughter more. She's a single mom and I remember one of the first things that really made a difference—I was retired; the boys had a bad flu and my daughter had to work. I could be there with them during the day, and get some laundry done, and we had some supper on, and just…help. I hadn't been able to do this when I was working.

My other son, has little ones—six and three. My son and daughter-in-law both work shifts and were wondering how they were going to manage because where do you get child-care that can fit the crazy schedules they have. But grandma was available. So that was the other thing; I was able to be there when they needed me.

Many months after I retired, a flyer came across my desk. It was for an art course at a local gallery. They were offering courses in medieval art history and experimental drawing. This allowed me to get back to my first love, which was art, and I registered immediately. I have been painting since then and loving it.

Our University president saw my work and liked it. He needed his official portrait done for the university and wanted me to do it. With support from my art instructor, I agreed. It turned out well and now hangs in the University Senate Chambers. Once I was retired, I also got involved in an election campaign working to elect a new government. I eventually joined our local riding association and was quite soon asked to be on the board. During the last federal election, I was very involved in the campaign, which resulted in the election of our candidate.

My Advice

- Just learn to enjoy and find stuff you like to do.

- Retire when you've still got the energy to create your next stage.
- Don't leave it too late, too long, because it's a transition; it's a major life transition.
- You don't know where retirement is going to go, but you can expect that it will look quite a bit like what you've done before.
- What you're doing might be different, but the approach, the way of being in the world, is still you.

Name: Len S.
Occupation: Teacher
Retirement Age: 54
Current Age: 64
Protirement Activities: **Political Activist**, New Careers/Jobs, Hobbyist; Travel Enthusiast

My Protirement Story

It wasn't long after I left my career in education that I was faced with the question..."Now what?" What was my purpose? What was I going to do with my life? I explored the Internet in search of an answer and investigated the possibility of going to Africa, on a mission, to assist the less fortunate. I was accepted by a group, but they wanted me to teach English. I understood their logic, but I was looking for a totally new experience. I wanted to help build houses, or work with my hands. I love teaching, but it just wasn't on my agenda any longer. Then a good friend of mine suggested that I run for municipal politics. Politics was never on my radar, but the issues of the day were of interest to me, so I decided to do that. I was a municipal councilor for two four-year terms.

After eight years of successfully serving the constituents of St. Catharines I wasn't sure what I wanted to do. One thing I knew for sure was that I loved interacting with people, so I put a resume together and dropped it off at every hotel in Niagara Falls. I was told that I was over qualified. Then I tried working in a call centre.

It lasted one day, and definitely was not for me. A friend, who owned a restaurant in Niagara-on-the-Lake, asked me to consider being a host at his restaurant. I did that for three years and ended up being a manager part-time for a short while. I loved the job because I had the opportunity to meet some very interesting people from around the world. After the restaurant job, I worked at a winery for one summer, hosting in the wine tasting room. An interesting thing about taking on any new experience, at an older age, is that you have a healthy dose of confidence that makes taking on new learning experiences that much easier. I remember when I started the job I didn't know anything about wine tasting, but because of my maturity and love for learning, I happily took on the challenge and gained new knowledge very quickly.

My wife and I have done a lot of travelling. We have been to Europe, South America and visited many parts of the USA and Canada. Hawaii is one of our favourite destinations. We hope to do more travelling in the future. I encourage everyone to read as much as you can because it opens your mind to new ideas and liberal attitudes towards life. Right now, I am between projects and really don't know what will be next on the agenda, but I do know it will be exciting and thought provoking. Opportunities just seem to happen to me. I am always willing to take on new and exciting challenges. You are never too old to learn, and life is designed to provide one experience after another, so get out there and embrace the multitude of opportunities. "Live, Love, and Learn" and never forget the value of "gratitude".

My Advice

- "Retire" isn't in my vocabulary. There is a whole new life awaiting you after retirement. Go after it and embrace it. If there is such a thing as "retirement", I believe it comes at the end of life."
- Never pass up an opportunity to learn and go about your life with kindness and gratitude.

CHAPTER 11: PROTIREMENT CATEGORY #7: HOBBYISTS

"When a door of opportunity closes,
many more doors open for you to proceed.
Remember; one of them is your hobby/passion.
You just have to look around and find that door."
Bharesh Chhatbar

Introduction

Baby Boomers are involved in an endless variety of exciting hobbies. The eight people I interviewed were active in a wide range of hobbies, including: knitting, organic fruit farming, stock trading, building computers, golf, photography, portrait painting, photographic history, reading, guitar playing, sailing, cycling, playing bridge, doing puzzles like Sudoku, and singing in choirs.

Facts about Hobbyists

Wikipedia defines a hobby as: "an activity, interest, enthusiasm, or pastime that is undertaken for pleasure or relaxation, typically done during one's own time."[22] Wikipedia divides hobbies into eight distinct categories. The following charts provide a sampling of hobbies within each category:

Indoor Hobbies

3D printing	Acting	Amateur radio	Baton twirling
Board games	Calligraphy	Candle making	Computer programming
Crossword puzzles	Dance	Drama	Fish keeping
Genealogy	Ice skating	Knitting	Leather crafting
Model building	Painting	Pottery	Soap making
Table tennis	Wood working	Writing	Yoga

Outdoor Hobbies

Archery	Astronomy	Baseball	Beekeeping
Bird watching	Bodybuilding	Camping	Driving
Fishing	Gardening	Hiking	Jogging
Kite flying	Letterboxing	Mountaineering	Road biking
Rock climbing	Shopping	Skydiving	Soccer
Swimming	Tai chi	Vehicle restoration	Water sports

Indoor Collection Hobbies

Action figures	Antiquing	Book collecting	Card collecting
Coin collecting	Comic book collecting	Record collecting	Stamp collecting

Outdoor Collection Hobbies

Antiquities	Flower collecting	Fossil hunting	Insect collecting
Metal detecting	Stone collecting	Rock balancing	Seashell collecting

Indoor Competition Hobbies

Badminton	Billiards	Bowling	Chess
Dancing	Fencing	Martial Arts	Poker

Outdoor Competition Hobbies

Archery	Beach Volleyball	Cycling	Fishing
Figure skating	Golfing	Squash	Tennis

Indoor Observation Hobbies

Fishkeeping	Learning	Reading	Videography

Outdoor Observation Hobbies

Amateur astronomy	Bird watching	Geocaching	Meteorology
People watching	Photography	Hiking	Whale watching

Engaging in hobbies meets many personal Protirement needs. A hobby gives an individual an activity to focus their energy on. By learning a new hobby, we engage and stimulate our brain, so hobbies can improve brain health. Hobbies are often done with other people, so they promote socialization and act as a deterrent to isolation and depression.

As we develop new skills or interests through a hobby, and become involved with a group of others who share the same interest, our personal identity can now become linked to that hobby. Our social status can also be connected positively to the hobby. If hobbies are physical in nature, they can also improve our physical health.

"Hobbyists" Protirement Stories

I interviewed eight Boomers who were Hobbyists as their primary Protirement activity. They ranged in age from 66 to 84. Their hobbies included knitting, organic farming, cycling, gardening, building computers, photography, history, reading, sailing and singing.

"Hobbyists" personal Protirement Stories follow.

Name: Barbara B.
Occupation: Secretary Treasurer Public Utility
Retirement Age: 53
Current Age: 68
Protirement Activities: **Hobbyist;** Travel Enthusiast; Community Builder

My Protirement Story

The adjustment wasn't too hard. I've always been a knitter. I am always, *always* knitting. It's my sanity, it's my soothing.

I volunteered at the Niagara Public Library and at the office of the hospital foundation. I worked a lot of hours in the office, volunteering. I can do those secretarial jobs that nobody else wants to do. When they moved to the new hospital, I stopped volunteering.

After my husband and I were both retired, we decided to move from Niagara-on-the-Lake to St. Catharines. Prior to moving, the de-cluttering and downsizing of all of our stuff took a couple months.

In those eighteen years living in Niagara-on-the-Lake, we both lost our parents, so we had sorted through our parent's things. We said, "We will not do this to our children." So, we did it, I would say, pretty drastically, this time.

We still have a few things of our son's. One son lives in Hamilton, so that was easier; every time we went to visit him, we dropped a box off. "It's yours; goodbye, see you next week." The other one has lived in the Middle East and is now in Massachusetts, so we couldn't do that to him. He's coming next month, and there are three boxes in the garage, waiting.

We've got two grandchildren in Hamilton, and two in Massachusetts. We're not called for babysitting duty and that kind of thing, because we're too far away. If it wasn't for Skype, I don't know how we'd manage, especially with the two in the States.

My Advice

- In the first year, say no to everyone. That will give you time to figure out your own life and what you would like to do.
- Stay busy.
- Stay active.
- Stay flexible so you can travel when you want to.

Name:	Barry K.
Occupation:	Entrepreneur; Corporate Executive
Retirement Age:	63
Current Age:	68
Protirement Activities:	**Hobbyist;** Corporate Side Hussles; Travel Enthusiast; Community Builder

My Protirement Story

I retired in 2011 and started doing corporate board work, despite my medical issues. Since then, I have been a director on a number of corporate directors' boards, which has helped me transition into my current work in patient advocacy. Typically, patient advocates are family friends of patients who help them get their medication or treatment. Unfortunately, these people are uninformed and don't know how to make things happen. Once the drug we needed became approved in Canada, I founded the Patients Association. I brought with me something nobody had ever seen before in patient advocacy in Canada. When we were fighting with the 10 governments across the country to get our medication approved and paid for, I had unlimited resources through donations. The medication we required was the most expensive medication in the world. I hired the number one medical media relations firm, the number one medical lobbyist, and the number one medical advocacy firm.

I ran it like a business; every Thursday at two o'clock, everyone had to be on that conference call. We were very structured, we delegated tasks to everyone, analyzed our results, and constantly modified our actions. We were very high profile. As a result, in 10 months we had over 500 media insertions, we were front page of the Toronto Star three times, front page of the National Post, and we were in McLean's Magazine. All of that was a result of my 35 years experience in business. We rose into the public eye and brought about change to government policy. We also began providing support to others who had the same disease.

I am also very involved in my fruit trees. I have a small grove or orchard of fruit trees. Everything is organic. The trees are probably 12+ years old. I bought all the equipment to make apple cider. I have equipment that mashes the apples, and equipment that presses the mashed apples. I have a 100 gallon stock pile of cider because I mix all the different varieties together. I use European bottles; pasteurize the juice, seal the jars, and boil them in water for 20 minutes. It was an absolute hit. My grandson took one sip of it, and I thought his eye balls were going to pop out. He loved it.

I have 18 blueberry bushes and about 65 to 70 fruit trees, including: pears, plums, cherries, and apples. I do everything organically using organic compost, organic seaweed, and organic fish fertilizer. I spend a lot of time down in the orchard. I also have beehives to help pollinate the trees each year. I have a tractor to help with the orchard work.

I still cycle a lot and we travel whenever we can. I did a lot of sailing and off-shore (ocean) sailing. Originally, we did lake sailing, but then my wife and I took some training in ocean sailing. It's a tremendous challenge, ocean sailing, when you are going someplace 250 miles away and you don't see anything except water. We enjoyed it and it's a great way of life. We love exploring the little towns and villages along the way, as we sail up and down the coast. We meet people with the same interests. We also sail in Europe and have gone to Spain and Morocco by way of the Mediterranean. I enjoyed taking cooking classes in both countries.

I have also been a volunteer on my Temple's Board of Directors and Chair for the Endowment Committee. I am still looking for different board directorships.

My Advice

- Whatever you're going to do, do it well, commit to it, and do it full-time.
- Balance your lifestyle.
- Follow your passions, be absorbed in them.
- Do things that make you happy.

Name:	Carlo S.
Occupation:	Restaurant Owner
Retirement Age:	61
Current Age:	83
Protirement Activities:	**Hobbyist;** Family Enthusiast

My Protirement Story

I arrived in Canada from Italy in 1966. The first few years I did various jobs in construction while I attended school to learn English. I also worked at General Motor for four years after that.

In 1968, I started my career as an entrepreneur, opening my first grocery store. After 3 years my wife and I opened a second store. Then, in 1973 we built a restaurant that we owned and operated along with our children, for 23 years. I retired from the restaurant in 1994. During that time I also dabbled in other businesses like owning/training race horses and trading in the stock market.

I learned other skills along the way, like how to use a computer, mostly because I needed to in order to run the restaurant. Once I retired and had more time on my hands, I learned how to use, format and build computers myself. It became, and still is, a hobby of mine.

I also took up gardening, but never really enjoyed it. I even went so far as buying a farm, with a couple of tractors, in Niagara-on-the-Lake. I wanted to grow grapes, but it didn't work out, so I sold the farm. I continued to garden, as I liked the fresh tomatoes and beans, but it's never been a passion for me.

You have to be passionate about what you are doing, to be successful, and you have to like people to be in business. In 1988, I had a serious car accident. It impacted on my enjoyment and ability to connect with people. Shortly after the accident, I had an old, out of town customer visit the restaurant. I hadn't seen him for a few years. He happened to be a physician. As we sat and had lunch together, he said, "Carlo, do you know something? You're not the same guy I remember you were." I told him about my accident and all the frustrations that went with it. At that time, it took 28 months to get an MRI in Canada. He called the Cleveland Clinic in Ohio on my behalf, and they booked me in for a MRI within the week. I drove down to Ohio, where they did a head to toe MRI. They booked me in without even asking how I was going to pay. They delivered prompt, excellent service. Although this was helpful in obtaining a fuller understanding of my diagnosis, I never fully recovered from the accident and finally was forced to retire in 1994.

I continued a few business interests after that time, keeping rental properties, as well as investments in the stock market. However today, at 82 years old, I am still trying to master gardening.

That's the story of my work life in Canada.

My Advice

- Enjoy yourself, travel, do what you feel like doing.
- Everyone has to do something.
- Exercise and eat healthy; make sure you take vitamins and minerals.
- Friendship and family are important, visit with people every day.

Name: Howie K.
Occupation: Counsellor
Retirement Age: 61
Current Age: 66
Protirement Activities: **Hobbyist;** Health Enthusiast; Life Long Learner; Family Enthusiast

My Protirement Story

I knew that I could retire with full pension, so I retired at 61. I made the decision to retire based on a number of things. I had health issues; heart by-pass surgery. That helps you see your mortality. I am in fine health now, but there was no way I wanted my tombstone to say: "I wished that I spent another day in the office." Health helped to see myself in a different light.

I thought of retirement as adjustment, because adjusting is going into a new situation or leaving an old situation. I never looked back for a second, never had regret, never said I wished I was still doing this. I felt like there was a nice ribbon on my career.

The adjustment was like being off for the summer and just not going back. I am good with vacation, so it was easy. I am good with down time, good with spontaneity, good with unstructured time.

There was lots of interaction in my job. I'm not the biggest social person, so I have to make an effort to be out there and find other environments to replace the social discourse that I had in my job. Going to the gym, taking courses, going out to lunch with friends, are ways of making that. It's like a thermostat in a house, when the temperature drops the thermostat kicks in. When I am not stimulated enough, I become restless or anxious, and that will stimulate me to seek out newness or opportunities.

Retirement helps me be free to spend time with my grandson. I don't think I am going to be a professional grandparent, though. Some grandparents like to be on call and see their grandchildren every day, but I don't think I would be satisfied with that. I want as much contact as I can have, but at the same time, I want to maintain my life and individuation from them.

During my retirement, I became more involved with my photography. It's the first time I actually saw myself as a photographer because people refer to me as that and people acknowledge my work in ways that I never thought possible. I got to see myself as a photographer.

My Advice

- Find ways to develop yourself as a person aside from your work, because the work is something that will eventually fall by the wayside.
- If you are the kind of person that needs to work or loves to work, then your work will continue far beyond the retirement age.
- Figure out what gives you pleasure in life and find ways to do it. Do you still want to make a contribution? Do you want to develop yourself? Do you want to contribute to the community? Taste, discover, experiment.

- Find ways to center yourself and live in the now, such as: yoga, meditation, and mindfulness practices.

Name: John B.
Occupation: Franchise Restaurant Owner/Marketing Executive
Retirement Age: 75
Current Age: 84
Protirement Activities: **Hobbyist;** Socializer; Life Long Learner

My Protirement Story

I worked until was 75. I loved working but had to stop due to health reasons, so I sold the McDonald franchises. Now, I spend my time reading books, magazines, newspapers, and a variety of educational pursuits, as well as socializing with friends and spending time with my granddaughter.

My Advice

- Keep busy.
- Get involved with activities.
- I believe 80 is the new 60.
- If you don't have health problems and love your job, why retire?

Name: Malcolm S.
Occupation: Social Development
Retirement Age: 67
Current Age: 70
Protirement Activities: **Hobbyist;** Community Builder

My Protirement Story

When I was 67, I was forced to retire when my government job was eliminated due to budget cuts. I took my personal possessions and was escorted out of the building. I called my wife and said, "Meet me for a coffee." I told her what happened. I was old enough to retire, I could apply for a pension. I took my settlement, accessed my pension, and officially retired as of June 2015. My wife had been thinking about retiring because her 65th birthday was coming, and I was trying to encourage her to retire at that point. Now, suddenly, I'm retired before her! "Just a minute, if you're going to be retired, I'm going to be retired, too!" she decided. So, she retired in August of that year.

After 47 years in the labour force, I got used to the idea of not working anymore. One thing I am still doing, as a volunteer, is the Atlantic Summer Institute on Healthy and Safe Communities. I was one of the founding board members in 2004 and am now the President of the board. We had a symposium on Child and Youth Mental Health Promotion in 2014 that attracted over 200 people. We're trying to be active year-round, in terms of promoting this work in the four Atlantic Provinces. So, I'm back tilting at that windmill where I started my career, childhood and youth, as a volunteer now.

When you retire, people ask, "Are you keeping busy?" Well, I suppose so. I mean, there are days when I read a book, or I may take a nap, so I'm not busy all the time, but I'm as busy as I want to be. I had been taking acoustic guitar lessons for a number of years, and I decided, about a year and a half ago, if I was ever going to learn how to play an electric guitar, I'd better start. So, I bought an electric guitar. That's what I'm working on now. In the winter-time, I play hockey with an old-timers' league. I really enjoy it and it's great exercise. When I first retired, it was summer-time in Nova Scotia. So there was a lot to do. I've got a small sailboat I bought the first year we moved to Halifax. I sail as often as weather permits. We've got a cottage down on the south shore that needs work. I had things to keep me busy, so I didn't really have a big adjustment. I think it went relatively smoothly.

My Advice

- After retirement, there will be time to do the things you enjoyed before retirement.
- Think about the things you never had a chance or time to do and spend time doing them.
- Find things that give you joy; live your life so you enjoy it.
- Put yourself first.
- Create your own structure for scheduling how you use your time.

Name:	Roger B.
Occupation:	Financial Analyst
Retirement Age:	60
Current Age:	75
Protirement Activities:	**Hobbyist;** Travel Enthusiast; Community Builder; Health Enthusiast

My Protirement Story

When I retired in October 2001 from the Financial Department of General Motors, I relaxed but also played a lot of tennis, which is one of my hobbies.

I am really interested in local history. In the early part of my retirement, I took a course at Brock University on the Welland Canals. For five years, I walked the length of the first three canals, taking pictures along the way of all the remnants, from Port Dalhousie out to Port Colborne. It was suggested that I put the pictures into a book, which I published in 2009. My book, H*istoric Welland Canals*, is currently sold at Lock 3, St. Catharines museum. Once the book was published, groups began asking me to speak at different functions, about the canal.

History, again, took my interest with the upcoming 100 anniversary of the War of 1812. I began by taking pictures of all of the re-enactments in Niagara and vicinity. This book was published in 2012, called *Niagara's War of 1812*.

My next venture was when I started to attend military history talks that were held at the St. Catharines Golf Club, where I met retired Canadian Army Lieutenant Colonel Ed Payment. Ed's sideline in retirement is doing battleground tours in Europe (France, Belgium Turkey and Italy). Ed invited me to take a tour in October 2012. Over the past four years I have gone on 10 battleground tours, taking pictures and developing souvenir books for the people on the tours.

My wife and I are avid gardeners so we are very busy during the spring, summer and fall. We have been fortunate to travel to different parts of Europe over the years. Recently, we have spent two months of the winter in Palm Desert, California. Our son and family come for part of the time' so it has become a family vacation. Friends have begun to rent places down there, so we have recreated our friendship group away from home.

My Advice

- Keep active
- Do something you love
- Make sure your spouse is supportive of what you do

Name:	Ticia D. M.
Occupation:	Marketing Advisor; Home Care Provider
Retirement Age:	70
Current Age:	72
Protirement Activities:	**Hobbyist; Life Long Learner**

My Protirement Story

After my dad died I received an inheritance and was able to buy my home in Port Dalhousie. I wanted to do something meaningful and ended up working at Pro Wellness providing home care to individuals. I went back to Brock University and began taking courses again, this time in Philosophy. I retired from Pro Wellness when I was 70, but still help out, where possible.

The concept of retiring has changed from the notion that retiring meant a 'Dolce Far Niente', or a wonderful life doing nothing....to continuing to work and possibly changing careers. Many of us have had to reinvent ourselves all over again.

That being said, if life has taught me anything, it is that you can always count on things to change. Retirement, or what passes for that, is just change, an adjustment. I like to play bingo, sing in choirs and in a barbershop quartet. I also play the ukulele.

I have always tried to find work that is like a hobby to me, to get paid for doing what I love. Then you never retire.

My Advice

- Release yourself from work slowly, and spike it with hobbies.
- Keep doing the things you love.
- Keep active in the community.
- Don't forget to smile.
- Keep your sense of humor.

CHAPTER 12:
PROTIREMENT CATEGORY #8:
CORPORATE SIDE HUSTLES

"A Side Hustle allows you to create new opportunities while having time for other endeavors."
Ellis Katsof

Introduction

Some of the Baby Boomers I interviewed had active careers in the corporate world and were still interested in maintaining contact with the corporate environment during their Protirement. They are doing so through Corporate Directorships, Angel Investing, and mentoring start-up businesses. These are all part-time or ad hoc initiatives, allowing plenty of time for involvement in other Protirement activities.

Facts about Corporate Side Hustles

The term "side hustle" has evolved with the Millennial generation. It is defined as: "A way to make some extra cash that allows you flexibility to pursue what you're most interested in. It can also be your true passion—a chance to delve into fashion, travel, or whatever it is you care about the most, without quitting your day job."

Based on interviews with former corporate executives, I have extended the definition of "Corporate Side Hustles" to reflect

Protirement activities this group of Boomers are involved in. I have redefined the definition in the following way: "A way to maintain a casual connection with the corporate world, volunteer, or earn additional income, and allow you the flexibility to pursue other Protirement activities you are most interested in."

"Corporate Side Hustles" Protirement Stories

I interviewed two people who were involved in "Corporate Side Hustles". They were 59 And 70 years old. They were also involved in a range of other Protirement activities, including: New Careers; Community Builders, Travel Enthusiasts, and Writers/ Performers. Their Corporate Side Hustles are on a casual part-time basis.

"Corporate Side Hustles" personal Protirement Stories follow.

Name:	Michael Adams
Occupation:	Marketing and Social Research; Author
Retirement Age:	Never
Current Age:	70
Protirement Activities:	**New Careers/Jobs; Corporate Side Hustles;** Writer; Travel Enthusiast

My Protirement Story

Having co-founded Environics in 1970, I appointed an Executive Director in 1990 who became president in 1995. I took leadership of the holding company for the Environics marketing and communications consulting companies and also took on the de facto role as professor emeritus at Environics, when I started writing books about social change in Canada and the United States.

In 2006, I read a Pew research study of attitudes of Europeans toward Muslims in Europe. This was after 9/11. The study included information on the attitudes of Muslims about living in Europe. I thought we should do a study like that in Canada, but I couldn't think of anybody who would hire us. So, I set up the Environics Institute for Survey Research. I hired Environics to undertake the survey for me and began looking for partnerships and funding from governments, foundations and NGO's...the model we still use today.

After the survey of Canadian Muslims, we surveyed urban Indigenous Canadians and most recently the Black community in the GTA. In these community studies, we partner with the community, making sure the community is fully involved in the design, execution, and roll-out of the research.

So, my career starts with establishing a business, adding complementary businesses over time. Following this, I wrote books about what our research was telling me; intended for a wider audience. And finally, most recently, I have become the patron of research my colleagues and I think should be undertaken. Perhaps this is the career story of someone who is compressing three generations into one.

By the time I am 75, I will probably be a grandfather for the first time and perhaps then ready to enter the adult phase of my life. I am 70, some days feeling I am only 50 and others closer to 80. Most days, I know I am 70, but with an awareness of my mortality. I read the paper every morning: first the sports, then the Obits, and finally the news of events in Canada and around the world. For another perspective, I devour the Economist and the Sunday NYT every week.

Until ten years ago, I took my health for granted, but over the last few years I have adopted a regimen of regular physical exercise. Body, mind, and spirit as the folks at the Y say. Of course, I enjoy opportunities to play tennis and golf with my buddies and my kids.

My Advice

- You should always be learning.
- You should always be working, but you don't have to punch a time clock.
- Build on your strengths and interests; do what is easiest and most fun for you but do it well.

Name: Nick D
Occupation: President & COO, Pharma Industry
Retirement Age: 55
Current Age: 59
Protirement Activities: **Corporate Side Hustles;** Travel Enthusiast; Community Builder

My Protirement Story

I was 55 when I retired. I had decided I was going to leave, I wasn't going to hang around. I wasn't going to do consulting. I had done this work for 25 years and it was now time to do something else.

I wanted to do something different. The first several months I said "no" to a lot of people who called me to do stuff, to do ventures, to do consulting. I didn't want to go back into the corporate world. My exit was pretty lucrative so I didn't have to work. I was fortunate. When I left, I wanted to get back into community life.

Even though we lived in Niagara, I commuted to the corporate office in Mississauga and wasn't involved in anything in Niagara. What quickly dawned on me was that I didn't have many connections where I lived. I got frustrated. It turned out to be a lot tougher than I thought, getting back involved with the community, because I didn't know the area.

When I was at Patheon, we built this development business where we got involved with these early stage bio-tech companies that needed support. I realized I wanted to do this locally. I decided to focus on Niagara and help build that type of network here. There wasn't an Angels Investors Network in Niagara so I joined the ones in Buffalo and Waterloo. I eventually helped to set one up in Niagara, called the Niagara Angels Investors Network. Through the Angels Investors Network, I got involved in early start-ups across Niagara.

I have been helping to build the eco-system in Niagara. Eventually, Innovate Niagara was started up as a Regional Innovation Centre, funded by the Ministry of Innovation to support early start-ups. I became an "Executive-In-Residence" for the Centre and provided mentorship services to early start-ups. It puts me in the heart of innovation in Niagara.

A Southern Ontario Angels Network has evolved and includes about 10 networks. I have been spending the past four years playing in that area and participating in building that eco-system. Innovation is where it's at, and we need to attract more knowledge based high value industry.

I sat on the Brock University Board for six years and was the Vice-Chair for a year.

I made two decisions when I retired: I wasn't going to work out of my home, and I had to have offices and places to go to keep a routine. I cut off ties from work which helped my transition.

I appreciated that I was home more. I didn't miss the corporate game stuff. I missed going to Europe, so we travelled more; did a lot of cruising.

My Advice

- Find out what you want to do.
- Don't do what you did before, do new things.
- Look for new ways to use your skills, strengths, knowledge.
- Be involved in the community, but find ways that build on your strengths.
- Take some time off.

CHAPTER 13: PROTIREMENT CATEGORY #9: TRAVEL ENTHUSIASTS

"Travelling -
It leaves you speechless,
then turns you into a storyteller."
Ibn Battuta

Introduction

Baby Boomers are embracing travel in their Protirement unlike any previous generation. They like adventure in their travels and are keen to explore the world.

Facts about Travel Enthusiasts

Baby Boomer travel trends are well documented by the travel industry, Statistics Canada, the Canadian Tourism Research Institute, CARP, AARP, and the media. In August 2016, Ontario Blue Cross reported that Canadian Boomers are expected to spend $35 billion dollars annually on pleasure travel, while the figure increases to $157 billion for American Boomers.[23]

Travel has changed from previous generations. Today, there are varied travel options compared to previous generations. Boomers have continually been reinventing travel experiences. Tourism now includes a variety of travel categories, meeting multiple travel interests and budgets. Travel categories include:

Adventure Tours

Boomers are physically fit and more adventurous than previous generations. They are exploring adventure tours, such as: mountain climbing, scuba diving, skiing, hot air ballooning, parachuting, and kayaking, to name a few.

Bucket List Tours

Baby Boomers have embraced Bucket List tourism in greater numbers since the 2007 movie, "Bucket List," with Morgan Freeman and Jack Nicholson. There is an endless number of "Bucket List," or "Must See" destinations. There are no agreed upon Top 10 destinations but here is a partial list of Bucket List destinations that are regularly mentioned in travel articles:

The Great Wall (China), Machu Picchu (Peru), The Grand Canyon (USA), The Pyramids of Giza (Egypt), Great Barrier Reef (Australia), The Sistine Chapel (Vatican City), Bora Bora (French Polynesia), The Eiffel Tower (France), Taj Mahal (India), Stonehenge (UK), Galapagos Islands (Ecuador), Mount Fuji (Japan), The Berlin Wall (Germany), Easter Island (Chile), The Arctic (Canada, Russia, Iceland, Greenland, USA), The Amazon River (South America), Serengeti National Park (Tanzania), The Himalayan Mountains (Pakistan, Nepal, India, Bhutan), Antarctica, The Holy Land (Israel), Petra (Jordan), and Mandalay (Myanmar).

Cargo Ship Travel

Boomers are beginning to explore this small unique market niche of travel. Only about 1% of the 29,000 cargo ships in the world offer this opportunity. They carry between 4 and 12 passengers per ship. The trips can vary from weeks to months, with stopovers for several days in each port along the way, while cargo is dropped off and picked up. While on board, you will experience a much quieter lifestyle than on a cruise ship. Activities will include hobbies like enjoying the sea, bird and dolphin watching, reading, writing, playing board games and cards with other passengers. On-shore visits during port stopovers will include unstructured touring.

Cruises

Boomers are having an impact on the way cruises are designed. Cruises have been adjusting their tour packages to accommodate Boomer interests, such as: healthy lifestyles, opportunities for stress free environments, ability to see multiple places along the cruise, and an increased environmental focus.

Cycling Tours

Boomers are health conscious and have embraced active travel options like cycling trips. The tourism industry is sensitive to this change and has been adapting cycling tours to include the aging Boomer by offering electric bicycles as well as traditional bicycles. Cycling tours are offered around the world in many different countries and settings.

Eco Tourism

Boomers' concern about the environment has opened up an entirely new travel opportunity. Some popular eco-tourism locations include: Galapagos Islands, Amazon rainforests, Norwegian fjords, The Himalayan Mountains, African jungles, Australia's Blue Mountains, wildlife of Alaska, and the glaciers of Antarctica.

Educational Tours

Boomers are embracing educational tours, where they can visit new settings and learn at the same time. Learning topics are quite varied but include topics such as: food and wine, birding, language, music, and photography.

Genealogical Tourism

Boomers are fascinated by their roots. These trips include visiting countries of origin. Trips often involve visits to towns and villages where ancestors grew up, and visits to relatives who are still living in those settings.

Medical and Dental Tourism

As Boomers age, medical needs increase. Medical Tourism has become a very large business in countries like Mexico, India, and Israel, where surgeries are far less expensive. Countries offer exciting tourism opportunities along with medical treatment at a cost far less than in the USA or Canada.

Multi-Generational Travel

Boomers are enjoying multi-generational trips. These trips include grandparents travelling with children and/or grandchildren. The trips are often planned around a life event like a birthday, anniversary, family reunion, or wedding. They can include travel by car, bus, train, plane, and cruise ships.

Mystery Tours

More adventurous Boomers are engaging in Mystery Tours; only knowing their airport departure location and not knowing the destination until they land.

Passion Tourism

Boomers have created a wonderful tourism industry focused around their passions. These tours include exploring passions, such as: food (e.g. Spain, Italy), wine (France, USA, Canada), scotch and whiskey (e.g. Scotland, Japan), beer (e.g. Ireland, Germany), and art and architecture (e.g. Europe).

River and Canal Cruising

Boomers are exploring unique locations by taking relaxing, romantic, river and canal cruises. These cruises are offered across Europe, Russia, Asia, and Egypt, and give Boomers the opportunity to explore the culture, food, wine, and architecture of the countries they visit.

Road Trips

Boomers enjoy hopping into their vehicles (cars, SUV's, Trucks, RV's) or onto their motorcycles and travelling across USA and Canada. They go from craft show to craft show, football game to football game, historic site to historic site, camp ground to camp ground, friends to relatives, etc. There are many travel clubs, such as: Harley Davidson Motorcycle Clubs, Airstream RV Clubs, RV Golf Club, and Passport America. Members enjoy organized trips and discounts across North America.

Solo Travel

As Boomers age they may find themselves single in the third chapter of their lives, either as a result of divorce or the loss of a partner/spouse. In the past, it has been costlier to travel as a single person. The travel industry has recognized this and is beginning to adapt by lowering the cost of travel for 'singles', changing the size of cruise cabins to accommodate singles, and offering more tours targeted at single Boomers.

Train Travel

Boomers have become reacquainted with train travel. Whether Boomers are travelling through the Canadian Rocky Mountains or Napa Valley in the USA for scenic relaxing travel, or across Europe or China on new, high speed trains, they are once again enjoying the experience of train travel.

Volunteerism Travel

Boomers have combined tourism and volunteerism as an opportunity to 'give back' while seeing the world. They support faith groups and non-profit NGO's to help implement projects in third world countries. Projects include such things as: building homes, hospitals, and schools, digging water wells, and providing dental, vision, and health services.

"Travel Enthusiasts" Protirement Stories

I interviewed five individuals who love travelling so much that they easily fit into the "Travel Enthusiast" Protirement category. They ranged in age from 67 to 83. There were many others who were interviewed who also enjoyed travelling, but as a secondary activity to their other primary Protirement activities.

"Travel Enthusiasts" personal Protirement Stories follow.

Name:	Doug H. R.
Occupation:	Director, Regional Government Department
Retirement Age:	62
Current Age:	83
Protirement Activities:	**Travel Enthusiast;** Community Builder; Family Enthusiast

My Protirement Story

I retired when I was 62. I had to be doing something after I retired, so I served as president of the Alzheimer Society and Foundation, and had the privilege of serving on a number of provincial, federal committees, boards, and councils.

When I first retired, I did a lot of public speaking to a variety of groups all over the country. Now, I speak more in Niagara. I was invited to write a column for the Senior Review, something I have done for the past 27 years.

I also did consulting across Canada and Japan. That was part of my plan for staying involved. One day, about eight years into my retirement, my wife said to me, "Doug, if you wanted to stay working why didn't you stay in your job?" After that, I started to back off of the work I was doing but stayed involved in a lot of boards and committees.

A lot of people say to me, "When are you going to slow down?" It's a very easy answer for me. I say, "I'm going to slow down when I can't do it."

I'm on the committee for the Age Friendly Network and on the board of Community Support Services of Niagara. I am also on the Welland Senior Citizens Advisory Committee. I am still trying to, as part of my retirement, be an advocate for seniors and trying to have some influence on how we're going to meet the growing needs of seniors. We need to talk about the tremendous contribution that seniors make, instead of the burden that seniors put on the health system. As consumers, seniors are the highest spenders; seniors provide thousands of hours in their volunteer work; seniors give thousands of dollars to charities; and when you look at a lot of the boards in the non-profit sector, many are filled with seniors.

I am 83 years old and I still feel I am making a contribution; my wife is 83 and she still volunteers in two Homes for the Aged.

We love going to the theatre and travelling, as well, particularly cruises. Cruising has been wonderful as we have gotten older. We went to Russia on a river cruise for our 50th anniversary. We've been to Sweden and Australia to visit our daughter. We take local day trips. I was a curler for 25 years and now golf two or three times a week.

What are those things that allow people to age in a positive way? I think one of them is staying busy, and there are many different ways to stay busy. My 42 year career as director of the Regional Niagara Senior Citizens Department, working with and for seniors, gave me a unique opportunity to observe first hand and learn ways that have helped me age in a positive way.

My Advice

- Like any other time in life, plan your retirement. You need to have a lot of interests outside of work so you can continue with them after retirement.
- Keep engaged with your family, if your family ties are strong. Strong family ties can really enhance your retirement.
- Volunteering can be a positive and rewarding experience that allows you to contribute to your community and country.
- I recommend exercise.

Name:	Evelyn B.
Occupation:	Teacher, Vice-Principal, Principal
Retirement Age:	53
Current Age:	68
Protirement Activities:	**Travel Enthusiast;** Caregiver; Hobbyist; Community Builder; Family Enthusiast

Protirement Story

After retiring and resigning from my board position on NCYC, I took a brief break from volunteer board work. In 2004, I was asked to join the governance committee of a newly merged children's mental health agency in Niagara (Niagara Children and Youth Services, NCYS). I stayed in that position for six years.

I was still on the provincial board (CMHO) at the time and was past president, so I did a lot of work around the province doing the accreditation presentations. I did a lot of travelling in the 2002 - 2003 year for CMHO. Retirement was relatively easy for me. It wasn't a difficult transition, possibly because I still had that involvement with CMHO. I knew I wanted to continue my volunteering in retirement. CMHO was still there and my local affiliations were still there, as well. And they have continued with Pathstone Mental Health, Clearview Community Initiatives, and Strive Niagara.

I have also continued to travel internationally (Portugal, Italy, South America, cruises) a lot. I often travel with a group of other teachers through a travel agency established by a retired teacher. I also travel with my sister and friends. I also have spent a fair bit of time, 13 trips, in Nova Scotia, taking care of a friend's business and pets while they travelled.

I have also been a caregiver for an aunt for 10 years, and that has taken up a lot of my time.

My hobbies include needlework and crocheting. I also enjoy reading and regularly attend an authors' series with a group of friends. I have also spent 40 years, with my sister, going to the theatre with the Mirvish Subscription series. I have continued doing that in my retirement. We also have a subscription at the Niagara Symphony. I am also part of the Retired Women's

Teachers Association. We meet three or four times a year. It's very social thing and it's nice to connect with colleagues that you have worked with. It gives me an opportunity to catch up with what everyone is doing.

Between the author's series, theatre, the music, volunteering, and travelling, I do keep very busy.

My Advice

- Have interests not related to work, ideally throughout your working career.
- Establish friendships and nurture them.
- Give back to the community.
- It's important to have a positive attitude, that the glass is half full!

Name:	Keith S.
Occupation:	Business Owner
Retirement Age:	57
Current Age:	73
Protirement Activities:	**Travel Enthusiast**; Community Builder

My Protirement Story

I was so lost it was unreal. For 6 to 12 months, I didn't know what to do with myself. Then, someone called me up and told me that he knew a young guy who was thinking about running for mayor in Burlington. Would I consider helping him? It was my first venture into community volunteering. Once he became mayor, he kept me involved in community work. He asked me to help organize a Mayor's Gala. Then, I was asked to help set up the Burlington Community Foundation. I joined the Tansley Woods Community Centre Committee and the Business Economic Development Council. Eventually, I joined the Transitions for Youth Foundation and helped set up the Youth Fest. I co-chaired the Burlington Performing Arts Centre Capital Campaign. Between

1993 and now, 23 years I have been volunteering in the community and have met some wonderful people, and have kept myself active.

I also love travelling. I own a large camper and travel in Canada and the States. Once a year, I go on a three-week road trip with three guys who I have been friends with for years. We go to three different football stadiums and cities each year. I also go on road trips with my partner. We have been to the east coast, the States, and other places across North America.

My Advice

- Keep busy, if you don't keep busy you can easily become a hermit.
- You need to get out and stretch your vocal chords.
- Life is so wonderful, get involved in community activities; the people you will meet will be wonderful and fulfilling.

Name:	Marty K.
Occupation:	Publisher, Consultant
Retirement Age:	64
Current Age:	67
Protirement Activities:	**Travel Enthusiast;** Hobbyist

My Protirement Story

I had been thinking about what I would do when I retired but neglected to plan for it other than financially. Just prior to retirement, we bought a diesel Volkswagen Golf and planned to take road trips because we loved to experience new places.

I was worried about what I was going to do in retirement. I knew that statistically many executives tended to become ill or die within two years due of the stress of having worked so hard in their jobs, then suddenly facing the prospect of having nothing to do. We began to plan road trips and I assumed that I would also continue to do some consulting. Within the first month of retirement, we took our first road trip down and up the east coast of the US. When we came home, we began to plan our second road trip to Newfoundland. I had a sudden realization that the stress I had been under in business was no longer there.

I also started reading four or five online newspapers a day and exercising regularly. Usually, I also plan one or two tasks or activities for the afternoon. I found myself slowing down and spreading out my activities throughout the week at a more relaxed pace.

There are changes in everything you do after you retire, including the relationship with your family, and particularly with your spouse. Our house was my wife's domain for many years, not mine. Fortunately, we had a seven-year period when we had our own company and we worked together from home. Accordingly, we were better prepared to deal with me being home all the time; however, I still had to be aware that this was her domain, so I had to ease into the picture. It was an important thing for me to recognize. It is difficult to prepare for all of those changes until you get there. You can think about them, you need to be aware that they happen, but until you're immersed in it, you don't really know what it's all about.

My Advice

- Don't try to over plan your retirement.
- Your planning could end up focussing on your previous lifestyle. You need to refocus on a new, retired lifestyle.
- Make sure you are active. The keyword for me is "active." It is too easy to become inactive.
- Be sensitive to the changes in your lifestyle that impact your relationship with your spouse.

Name: Peter F.
Occupation: Public Sector Executive
Retirement Age: 60
Current Age: 67
Protirement Activities: Political Activist; Hobbyist; **Travel Enthusiast; Community Builder;** Writer; Family Enthusiast

My Protirement Story

I retired in 2010 from my job as the Central Ontario Field Unit Superintendent where I led a 250 FTE organization that included the Trent Severn Waterway, the Georgian Bay Islands National Park and Bethune Memorial House. This position concluded a varied career that included working as a Co-op Manager in Ulukhaktok, NTW, varied positions with Indigenous and Northern Affairs Canada, setting up a NFP on Municipal – Aboriginal Relations and the start up of three pan Canadian heritage programs with Parks Canada.

Throughout my career, I have been involved with different not-for-profit boards. Following my retirement, I served on the board of the Art Gallery of Peterborough, the Peterborough Regional Health Centre and a grassroots economic development organization, the Community Opportunity Innovation Network. For a couple of years I also continued to serve on the United Way fund raising Cabinet.

Post retirement has opened up opportunities for more explicit political commentary. These have been in the form of open letters with former colleagues to government regarding service reductions on the Trent Severn Waterway and Park Canada's abdication of its legislative responsibilities for environmental protection. I have had fun engaging the local MP to replace rural post boxes, and in the process, tormenting Canada Post with a neighbourhood petition and various emails. I have also written to Ministers proposing a set of measures for heritage conservation in the federal domain.

I also took the opportunity to learn some Spanish, following an online Spanish course for about a year. This interest partly inspired extended travel in Argentina and Chile with my wife, during which I took some immersion courses and we hiked in Pantagonia. My retirement also enabled me to complete a major landscaping project, implementing the planting plan and then further expanding the garden. This of course included a vegetable patch which then evolved into canning and other cooking projects. Local food production inspired me to return to a vague desire, discussed with my sister over the years, to collect and consolidate family recipes. This project morphed into a 260 page family cookbook, tentatively called, *Frood on Food, Sort of...* It is like a memoire, disguised as a cookbook.

I have developed an interest in long distance walking. My first experience, when I was 50, was a month long pilgrimage walk in northern Spain. After I retired, I did another pilgrimage walk in France; 400 kilometres on my own and another 200 with my wife. I find this type of travel to be an intimate, convivial and reflective way to experience landscapes and other cultures.

My wife and I are regular travellers. Aside from the usual southern junkets, we have gone on a number of extended trips: Russia, Thailand, Iceland, South America and a trip to various places in the Dolomites and northern Italy. Future travel projects include the grand tour of North America in a camper van and an extended trip in Australia, Tasmania, and New Zealand. We are discussing other extended walks in Europe and the UK and have an ever expanding list of possible treks. We plan to do as much active travel as we can while we are still healthy.

We also enjoy bike touring. Our first trip while working was a Tour du Lac St. Jean in Quebec. For the last couple of years, we have connected with a network of riders and have done a couple of trips with them. One was from Peterborough to Prince Edward County, and then back to Peterborough. Last summer we travelled along the Erie Canal in New York with the group and then, on our own, did another trip from Oshawa to Niagara-on-the-Lake, returning to Oshawa by bus and train. We may also organize a group tour in Quebec, likely along the south shore from Quebec to Rimouski.

When I get closure on the *Frood on Food, Sort of...* project, I will start on another one, *Who was Oren Frood?* The point of departure will be the Orens, my father and grandfather but it will really be a consolidation of family history, capture fragmentary family information (supplemented by secondary sources) on my two uncles who died in WW1, include sections on hockey history as well as documenting my grandmother's family. The real audience for both of these projects is our grandchildren.

We are currently spending a lot of time in Kuujjuaq Quebec, Nunavik's largest community on the shore of Ungava Bay. Our time in Kuujjuaq gives us unique opportunities including hiking at the Pingaluit Crater last summer and this August, hiking in the Torngat Mountains. While living in Peterborough, my wife worked from our home as a consultant for a Nunavik organization but has since accepted a full time position in Kuujjuaq. We have sold our house in Peterborough, established ourselves in a condo in Toronto and have purchased a condo in Ottawa, which is now under construction. In the summer of 2018, my wife will retire and we will settle in Ottawa to be closer to our son and his family.

Grand parenting is a joy. We look forward to bouncing between Ottawa and Whistler, where our grandchildren live with their caregivers. Ottawa will provide a base for our travel projects. As a larger city, it provides access to public archives, which I need for my history project and has varied Spanish courses and other courses. I am looking forward to conclude our downsizing and to settle again in a community where I can participate in community based organizations.

My Advice

- Be physically active.
- Stay connected and engaged with the community.
- More fully explore existing interests; actively develop new skills.

CHAPTER 14: PROTIREMENT CATEGORY #10: COMMUNITY BUILDERS

"We make a living by what we get. We make a life by what we give."
Winston Churchill

Introduction

Baby Boomers are embracing a wide variety of volunteer work, more than any other age group. They are volunteering on boards; doing direct service work in community agencies for children, families, seniors, the homeless, and others; joining advocacy groups; supporting community recreation and sports organizations; participating in church, synagogue, and temple activities; fund raising; advocating for the preservation of heritage sites; volunteering for international organizations; and more. The list of volunteer opportunities is almost endless. At the root of this activity, are thousands of people making a difference in their communities, so I have labelled this Protirement category, "Community Builders."

Facts about Community Builders

Thirty nine percent of Canadian volunteers, older than 55, contribute the most volunteer hours of all age groups according to a survey done by Volunteer Canada in 2013.[24] This makes Boomers the largest age group among volunteers. Boomers, having grown up during the social change and civil rights movements of the 60s and 70s, appear to have continued their social commitment through their volunteer work. Many different motivators underlie Boomers volunteering. They include an opportunity to:

- Make a meaningful contribution;
- Continue using their skills;
- Pursue interests;
- Meet new people; and
- Have time to pursue other interests.

Volunteer Canada describes six different types of volunteers[25]:

The Groupie: These volunteers thrive on the camaraderie of a group and like to have fun and get results.

The Juggler: These volunteers are dynamos who enjoy giving their time to a variety of organizations.

The Cameo Appearance: These volunteers have an unpredictable lifestyle and cannot be a regular volunteer.

The Rookie: These volunteers are cautious but they've started to think it's time to give back.

The Roving Consultant: These volunteers are incredibly focused and want to volunteer their specialized skills.

The Type A: These volunteers are multi-tasking leaders who say "yes" often and mean it.

If you would like to determine which type of volunteer you are, Volunteer Canada has a short online survey you can complete to determine which of the above six categories best fits you. It can be found at: https://volunteer.ca/blog/take-volunteer-quiz-remplissez-le-questionnaire-des-b-n-voles.

Boomers volunteer in a wide range of non-profit organizations and settings, including:

• Advocacy	• Animal Care	• Civic and International
• Children, youth, and family	• Social and Community Services	• Sports and Recreation
• Culture and Arts	• Environmental	• Hobbies
• Hospital and other health settings	• Public Safety	• Religious

Within the above settings, Community Builders take on a variety of roles, including governance roles, such as sitting on Boards of Directors, Committees and Advisory Committees; Direct Service, such as working directly with clients, running programs and events, etc.; Fund Raising; Advocacy; Volunteer Advisors and Community Development.

"Community Builders" Protirement Stories

More interviewees were active as Community Builders, both as their primary and secondary Protirement activity, than any other Protirement activity. Sixteen interviewees were Community Builders as one of their primary Protirement activities, while another 34 were Community Builders as a secondary Protirement activity. Community Builders ranged in age from 55 to 86. Five Community Builders sat on Boards of Directors or Advisory Committees, 2 were involved in fund raising and nine were engaged in direct service activities.

The "Community Building" personal Protirement Stories follow.

Community Builders: Board of Directors and Advisory Committees

Name: Bonnie E.
Occupation: Government Executive
Retirement Age: 59, 66
Current Age: 72
Protirement Activities: **Community Builder**; New Career; **Caregiver;** Hobbyist; Health Enthusiast; Family Enthusiast

My Protirement Story

My second husband had a business based in Toronto and wanted to move his business down to Montreal for a few years. So, after my retirement, we moved to Montreal. We bought a condo in Old Montreal. My first stage of retirement was just enjoying downtown Montreal, reigniting with some of my old friends from high school days, and living a wonderful life. I had gotten into golf and skiing while we were working and continued that while in Quebec. I had joined an exercise club for fitness, as well.

After we returned to Toronto, I had heard about a Board of Director's opening for a Local Health Integrated Network in Toronto, and I applied for it. I figured that was a good project to have in my retirement and was appointed to the first board. I was a Director of the Board for about two years until the CEO had left and I was asked to leave the board and become an interim CEO. I was 65 at the time and my husband was still working, so I agreed to do it. It was supposed to be for six months but I ended up doing it for about a year.

We sold our Quebec country house and bought one north of Toronto for our retirement. We skied and golfed on the weekends and worked hard during the week in Toronto. My husband decided to retire and leave his business to his son. We retired, my second time, on the same day. We went up north and gave ourselves a big party. We eventually sold our house in Toronto and bought a condo. We also became grandparents around that time, so we wanted to maintain a base in Toronto. I got approached by the hospital and LHIN up north, but decided that it was time to stop working again.

During those two years, we golfed, skied, biked, walked, went to variety shows and festivals, gardened, spent time with friends, got into canning and making jams, and were grandparents to triplets. After two years, my husband got sick and we had to be in Toronto often for his treatments. We bought a larger condo in the same building as our first condo and still managed to spend some time up north, although we realized it would not be our retirement home as planned.

Now, our time is spent mainly in Toronto. I don't do anything in the way of business or volunteering any more. My husband can't golf any longer because his vision is limited due to his cancer. I guess you can call me a caregiver now because he is dependent on me. We still travel to Florida in the winter but they are short trips because of my husband's treatments. We also go to Vancouver to visit my husband's family. Socially, we still see our friends but we don't hang out to the bitter end and party all night long. But we still stay in touch with our friends both in Toronto and up north. We lead a quiet but pleasant life.

My Advice

- Stay close to your family; they can be such a source of joy. It's such a source of joy, being around grandchildren, never under estimate it.
- Look after your health, life is unpredictable.
- Don't stay in your job just because it pays well; always keep an open mind as to careers and what they're doing. If you're not happy, find a job where you are happy.
- Relationships are very important.
- Stay active; make room for fun in your life while you are working.
- Keep a very positive outlook on life, don't sour over things. Attitudinally, it's really important to look on the good side of things.
- Don't get stuck in one house, or community, don't be afraid to change your life, throughout your life. I bought

and sold 10 properties, both city and country, across two provinces, and lived in and loved them all!

Name: Catherine M.
Occupation: Infection Control Expert
Retirement Age: 47
Current Age: 63
Protirement Activities: **Community Builder;** Family Enthusiast

My Protirement Story

At 47, I had health concerns and decided to retire, so I returned to Niagara. That was 16 years ago. It gave me the opportunity to change the way I was living. I had been around the world twice and had enough of travelling; it was time to come home. I stayed with my parents for a year, figuring out what I was going to do.

My dad was retired and had always done volunteer work. At the time, there were about 60 refugees from Columbia, Rwanda, and Tibet coming across the border in Fort Erie a day. My parents went down to the border daily to help the refugees. There was an obvious opportunity to put a system in place to deal with the disorder of settling the refugees that was occurring . The government decided to rebuild the border crossing building. Leading a group of dedicated volunteers we approached the manager and suggested they divide the building in half, with a locked door between the one side of the building where the border crossing guards were doing refugee processing and the other side where the refugees could be housed as a Welcome Centre. I helped redesign the new building so that it included a Welcome Centre. The regional government agreed to put in a child care center. We applied for funding to provide a medical unit there, as well. It was the top Trillium award for 25 years. When refugees arrive at this center, they always remember their time there.

We then developed a community reference group and began planning for a Community Health Centre (CHC) in Fort Erie. It involved extensive lobbying of the provincial Minister of Health. Eventually, the minister approved funding for Fort Erie. The MPP's in Niagara Falls and St. Catharines wanted similar CHC's in their communities. Community reference groups were already planning for CHC's in their communities. Funding eventually was approved for all three communities.

I was on the board at Family and Children's Services (FACS) at the time. I was quite active on that board. Kids were my world. I have 37 nieces and nephews, and 22 great nieces and nephews. I was also on the board of the Migration Center at the Fort Erie Bridge. There was a person who headed up a literacy program and had a book club and invited me to join it. It was a social club for women who enjoyed literature. I joined a Niagara wide book club. I then began to pull people together to use evidence to plan for the vitality of Niagara. This effort involved a community planning process with community stakeholders, which eventually was called Niagara Connects.

I kept hearing about kids, poverty, and domestic abuse while I was a board member with FACS. The region was about to do another study about this issue. FACS met with the region and talked about doing a joint project. I heard the same story at another community table, again. I started to pull a group of people together to talk about the lack of social planning in Niagara. We no longer had a District Health Council, and did not have a Social Planning Council. We needed to put our heads together to plan together with evidence for the vitality of Niagara because we didn't have reliable, valid data and research that was Niagara specific. Niagara Connects evolved out of those discussions.

During this time, along with my siblings, I also spent time as a care giver for my elderly parents.

My Advice

- The choices you make in your earlier life, the way you think, and the way you listen, and the way you act, will affect your retirement.

Name: John S.
Occupation: Business Owner
Retirement Age: 62
Current Age: 63
Protirement Activities: **Community Builder;** Health Enthusiast; Life Long Leaner

My Protirement Story

I stopped working professionally and just carried on my volunteering so the transition has been easy. My wife has been on and off of work because of her cancer. I would go with her to medical appointments. Also, I have been taking courses at the School of Philosophy for the past four years. That allows me to think about life. In addition to that, I chaired a business committee for the City of St. Catharines while I was still working. I was also a chair of a planning task force that led to the building of the Garden City Arts Centre. I was also on the community advisory committee of the Niagara Health System. I go to the gym at least four times a week.

In retirement, I now surround myself with active thinkers. They don't have to necessarily be positive people, but people who are active in their thinking process. I like to help people, I mentor people now. When I was Chair of the Niagara Workforce Planning Board, I set up new immigrants with a mentor and carried on mentoring a young woman from China. We met for eight weeks at Starbucks.

I have two kids, a son who is 30 and has a Ph.D., and a daughter, 28, who works for Positive Living.

My Advice

- Know who you are and what drives you, what's important to you.
- Serve others.
- Have good relationships with other people.
- It's important to be loved, to be a good friend.
- Always be a student.

Name: Mike T.
Occupation: Regional Government CAO
Retirement Age: 62
Current Age: 63
Protirement Activities: New Careers/Jobs; **Community Builder**; Philanthropist; Family Enthusiast

My Protirement Story

I think the loss of a sense of relevance can be most challenging. As a CAO, I liked the recognition but didn't have a real hunger for it or for the individual profile that came with the job. In fact, I had to get used to the attention that came with the role. So, it was easier for me during the transition period once I retired and no longer had the profile.

Many other retirees that I talked to found—I call it the relevance phase—that they still had a need to feel relevant. For some, it was the profile and attention that filled this need. I kept good friendships with a lot of the CAOs in Ontario and can remember one of them saying, shortly after he retired, "It is amazing how quickly people forget you!" That's something I think everybody needs to be aware of and watch out for.

After I retired, I took the entire summer to relax. In the fall, the President from Niagara College approached me to fill in as VP of Administration at the college on a limited contract basis. I stayed in that position for seven months but it felt too much like the 24/7 of a full time job and the need to give 120%. My time wasn't really mine, and it felt too much like what I had just left. It convinced me that I needed to find something that was more casual.

I do some part time consulting and business development.I am also on the Board of Directors for the Housing Services Corporation for Ontario. I was on the local United Way board until this year. Last year, I was asked to join the National Board for Special Olympics Canada. It's an interesting group of people from across the country. Some pretty amazing people with high profiles from the sports and corporate world are on it. As well, with our daughter being a Special Olympic athlete, we have had a lot of involvement in Special Olympics sports.

When I retired, I didn't want a big retirement party, but there was a very nice casual gathering and those who came were asked, in lieu of bringing gifts, to donate to a family fund that we established to support activities for individuals with intellectual disabilities. The resulting fund allows us to support a number of local causes in addition to our direct volunteer support

Be prepared for the unexpected when it comes to the transition period. When I retired, I was very physically active and doing things around the house. I had more time to be physically active but I was suddenly having trouble sleeping. I couldn't understand it! When I was working, I would put my head on the pillow and be gone for the night. I think I was always emotionally and mentally exhausted at the end of the work day, whereas now that I am retired I am physically tired but, mentally, not so much. I went through a period where it was driving me crazy, I didn't expect that as a retirement issue! It took some time to get over it, probably six months before I was sleeping well again.

My wife retired two years before me. When I retired, we suddenly were getting in each other's way. I was spending more time around the house, and being used to a certain pace she started calling me, "Uber Mike". Even though I wasn't on a deadline anymore, there was always this sense of urgency. My wife had two years to wind down from her demanding job and had been able to adjust to a different pace while I was just beginning to adjust. It would drive her crazy that I had to have everything scheduled with a deadline.

I was fortunate, while working, to have an administrative assistant who was always excellent at making sure that my day was properly scheduled. She managed my calendar completely. In the first year after I retired, it was announced at one of our board meetings that the United Way kick-off breakfast would be on September 12th. That was easy to remember because it was my birthday. But I totally missed it!! I didn't think I would need to put it in my calendar. Two days later, when it dawned on me, I had to call the Executive Director and apologize for being AWOL. I had to learn to manage my own calendar and make sure I had everything entered into it.

I can't say that I miss all of the day-to-day work that I did but I do miss the interactions, and I miss the shared sense of accomplishment with the talented people that were a part of my work family . I try to keep in touch with some of that family but, as far as the work I did, that's a part of my life that's finished.

We are fortunate to have our kids and five grand kids who are all local. I wouldn't say we spend a a great deal more time with them now that we are retired but the time we do spend is more enjoyable and relaxing because we no longer have to worry about cramming it into our tight work schedules.

My Advice

- Whatever you think you are going to do after you retire, start doing some of it before you retire. Whether it's volunteer work, sports activities, travel, try to build small amounts into your schedule.
- Accept that one chapter of your "book of life" has ended and it may be difficult to try and hang on to it. Commit yourself completely to the new and exciting chapter – one that can be fulfilling and rewarding – but perhaps in a very different way .
- Find something to give yourself a sense of feeling needed, a sense of accomplishment, and a sense of relevance. Test it out before hand to see if it gives you what you need, and if it doesn't, be prepared to find something else.

Name: Pamela M.
Occupation: Secretary
Retirement Age: 60
Current Age: 86
Protirement Activities: **Community Builder**; Writer

My Protirement Story

Before I retired from a Secretarial job I had been doing for about 40 years at a local paper company, I was offered volunteer work as secretary of the local Heritage Committee. This is a committee which is appointed by Council and whose mandate it is to advise Mayor and Council on matters as they pertain to the heritage of their community. I have also represented our committee on the Regional Culture Committee, local BIA, Tourism Committee and Downtown Façade Committee.

As my interest grew in this subject, I could see the wisdom in heritage preservation and joined the committee as a member the following year. My interest, understanding and passion for heritage has done nothing but grow over the years, and for the past 30 years it has taken up most of my time. For 10 years my involvement covered our entire region of 12 municipalities, and this gave me an opportunity to meet and work with many of the people in the area who were also involved in this cause. Over the years I have written many articles on heritage preservation, given speeches on the subject, spoken at conferences and, on a daily basis have tried to assist with any problems which have arisen. Today I am attempting to pull back on some of the work – but I am finding that difficult to do!

In my own municipality we now have over 50 sites designated under the Ontario Heritage Act, which is an outstanding number for the size of the community. We also have a downtown business area which is undergoing a total revitalization.

People are beginning to realize that our heritage – built, cultural and natural, is important. It is what gives our municipalities their uniqueness; once we have lost a building or site we can never get it back! When we first started this committee in the 1980s, it was an uphill climb constantly --- nobody seemed to care. Now, the politicians, developers and residents are beginning to understand the importance of retaining our past for future generations to appreciate. Our committee is consulted about demolitions, development projects and many aspects of changes and expansions in the community. The Welland Canal, cycling and heritage are the three attractions in my community which bring in visitors to our growing tourism market.

The stone building where I made my home until recently, is a designated building. It was an old flour mill, at one time associated with the Maple Leaf Milling Company. It has since been converted to a new use for businesses along with 20 apartment units. This is what we call *"adaptive-reuse"* – that is, a new use is found for an old building instead of it being demolished and all the building materials sent to the landfill. This is obviously not a good use of our resources and is a threat to a clean environment.

I have been fortunate enough to have been recognized with many awards over the years.... 2003 Lifetime Achievement Award, 2014 Niagara Builder; in 2016 I was honoured with the Niagara Woman of the Year Award; in 2002 I received the Queen's Golden Jubilee Medal; in 2011 the George & Olive Seibel Award for outstanding contribution to the preservation of the history of Niagara.

There isn't a day that goes by that I don't receive a heritage question from someone – somewhere! I don't always have the answers but I do my best to refer them to someone or some source which can assist in furthering their understanding of heritage.

I have learned that when you leave the work you have devoted your life to, it is important to move on to something new. A friend of mine commented to me one day *"you have had an interesting life"* – and I thought about this! I had all these life experiences in my head – at the time of living them I felt that it was a huge struggle! But I am now 87 – I need to write these experiences down – I need to write a book – which I have underway! It is about growing up, learning, taking responsibility, loneliness, doubt, marriage, becoming a parent, and women who find a way to grow through adversity.

My Advice

- Find something you love.
- Find something that you believe in, something that you can commit yourself to, and do it!

Community Builders: Fund Raisers

Name:	Frank L.
Occupation:	Former newspaper publisher, business owner, Angus cattle breeder and real estate agent.
Retirement Age:	59
Current Age:	78
Protirement Activities:	**Community Builder;** Travel Enthusiast; Health Enthusiast; Family Enthusiast

My Protirement Story

I've always found it rewarding to help non-profit agencies and community organizations in Niagara. I joined the Niagara Falls Rotary Club for five years, shortly after my retirement. I've also been a director of the Branscombe Family Foundation since 1999. Here, I've helped commit funds to health, education, and social well-being in Niagara, thanks to the generosity of its two founders—Frank and Mildred Branscombe.

I was appointed by the Province to the Niagara Parks Commission in 2000, and was pleased to serve for six years. Later, I acted as co-chair of the Niagara Health System Foundation, but left in 2007 when I began to experience some serious mental health issues. Thankfully, following various treatments and the support of my family, I made a complete recovery by 2011. After that experience, I was asked to join the Pathstone Foundation's "Mending Children's Minds Campaign" as Honorary Chair. If I hadn't gone through a few years of mental illness, I probably wouldn't have become involved with Pathstone or had the urge to become an advocate for mental health. I'm a strong believer in trying to eliminate the stigma surrounding mental illness by talking about my own experiences.

Spending time with my wife and family, and particularly our grandchildren, is the most important part of my life right now. Friends take on more importance as we grow older and I'm blessed to have many. I began playing golf back in high school and still play golf with a bunch of my friends, although a bit less often lately. Writing also continues to be a personal enjoyment.

For some, the word “retirement” is “just waiting for the call” or “sitting around, vegetating and watching TV.” To me, that isn’t functioning. Making a positive and meaningful impact in the lives of my family, friends, and community will always be my goal.

My Advice

- People should ask themselves: “What am I doing outside of work and family?” If the answer is not much, then they should begin doing something, whether it is volunteering, sports, or hobbies, as long as they have interests other than work and family.
- If not now, then when?

Name:	Greg W.
Occupation:	Corporate CEO
Retirement Age:	64
Current Age:	65
Protirement Activities:	**Community Builder,** Caregiver; Travel Enthusiast; Family Enthusiast

My Protirement Story

When I retired from Algoma, everyone assumed that I would consult or go for another job. I had the best job in the world, was well paid and loved it, why would I retire to get another job? There are lots of people who hate their job and are counting down the days to retirement, but I wasn’t in that situation. I was 64, 35 years with the company, and had started to think about it a year before. I didn’t have a big plan. A year before I retired, I started thinking about it, and finally decided I should do it.

In the first few months after I retired, we did a lot of travelling. Some of it was left over from my work because I still had a few obligations related to work that included some travelling. We were able to act as tourists while I completed some final responsibilities by attending a couple of meetings in Seattle and Newcastle,

England. Right up until the summer, we had a lot of things going on so there wasn't any worry of not being busy.

The pace for me is a lot slower now. I was usually at work by shortly after 7:00 am. I am now able to take my time in the morning, have a coffee, stay in bed, and read the paper, it's very relaxing. I then get on with my day. The other thing I got involved with very shortly after I retired was when the mayor called me up and invited me to lunch. They were just getting off the ground with the Welland Canal Fallen Workers memorial for the 137 workers who lost their lives building the Welland Canal. He asked me if I'd head up the fundraising. So, in June 2015, I got involved in that.

It was a good transition for me. I was able to leverage my contacts, and go and talk to people I knew in the industry about something I had a passion for, and it kept me a little connected. It helped ease me out.

Being at home, every day, was challenging, probably more for my wife than for me. The only thing she said was, "I don't like grocery shopping with you." I was there, grabbing things, and pushing the cart, and getting in people's way, so we don't often go grocery shopping together any more. That was our biggest challenge, and it was a pretty easy one. We both like to travel. We have travel plans coming up in the future and would like to do as much as we can while we are healthy.

I had a lot of friends in the company and the industry. It's definitely harder to keep in contact. I miss that. We play hockey every Friday morning, so I see a lot of the guys I know and it keeps me linked to work friends. In hockey, when they knock me down now, they don't pick me up as they did when I was CEO. That's the only difference.

I spend a lot more time with our family now. Our grandson is four years old. We spend a lot of time with him. He has mild Autism and we help out a lot with him. We are happy that we can offer that. One of his weekly sessions is at our house to give him some variety in settings.

Fortunately, for us, we have lots of interests. We have family, we like to travel, we like to garden, and we like to get involved in volunteerism in the community.

My Advice

- You have to have interests that allow you to be happy with your day when it's over.
- Sitting around in retirement and sitting on a chair watching TV your whole life is not good.
- It's important to have a few sets of friends with the same interests and things you like to do together.

Community Builders: Direct Service

Name: Art W.
Occupation: Teacher, Vice-Principal, Principal, Superintendent
Retirement Age: 59
Current Age: 82
Protirement Activities: **Community Builder,** New Career/Job; Family Enthusiast

My Protirement Story

I remarried on June 26 1994 and retired on June 30 1994. I went into marketing for Bazaar Novelty. In 1995 I was recruited to be President of a faltering company in the Niagara tourist areas. Within a year, we shut down the business. At the same time, we started a couple start–up internet companies where we tried, until 1998, to make a viable business when the 90's internet bubble was selling sizzle with no steak.

From 2001- 2005 I was the founding chair for Contact Niagara, a not-for-profit access-to-service organization for families with children with disabilities. From 2002 to 2005 I volunteered as a Board member for the start-up of the Early Years program in the Niagara Region.

I got more involved in Rotary. My wife and I were co-membership chairs for the Rotary District 7090 in 1997. In 2003, I took a Group Study Exchange team to India. In the same year I was nominated to become the District Governor and began the training program to assume the position in 2005. I worked with 75

Clubs in New York State and Southern Ontario during my year as District Governor. From 2005 to 2016 I was involved with all of the committees at the District level, but my primary focus was the District 7090 Rotary Foundation Committee. For three of those years I was the Foundation Director where we raised about $300,000 annually for the Annual Fund and $100,000 annually for Rotary International's "End Polio" program. Between 2015 and 2016 I held a position with the Rotary Foundation for Eastern Canada. I have also been involved with a number of Rotary projects in Bulgaria

In addition, my wife and I have travelled extensively and we have a condo in the Naples area in Florida. With 5 children and 8 grandchildren, two families, in the US and three in Canada, there is never a shortage of opportunities to be involved with our family.

My Advice

- Retirement doesn't mean quitting.
- Keep active.
- Be involved in the community.

Name:	David E.
Occupation:	Social Worker, Consultant
Retirement Age:	65
Current Age:	82
Protirement Activities:	**Community Builder;** Family Enthusiast

My Protirement Story

I retired when I turned 65, by slowing down my consulting over a year or so. I stopped hanging out my consulting shingle and let it die off by the end of the year. I didn't have a real formal plan, but I had a fear of sitting around and doing nothing. I knew I had to be doing something. I met someone who introduced me to an organization called CESO (Canadian Executive Service Organization). I contacted CESO 16 years ago and am still volunteering for them today.

To be honest, I didn't look forward to retiring. The idea, the myth that you're just going to sit around and do lovely things all day like playing golf, that kind of thing, is strange and not very realistic. You have a bit of that when you initially retire, the sense of just chucking the load, that's a nice feeling. I dickered around in my head about just doing a bit of consulting here and there, that kind of stuff and so on, but the CESO volunteering took over and filled my needs, so I didn't have to do something else.

I am 82 years old today and don't know what I am doing here, it comes faster than you think, finding yourself in that group is very odd. To this day, I like it when I meet someone who is older. I look for people in their nineties.

I am now doing only administrative work for CESO. I stopped doing international trips once I turned 80. I have had 24 assignments in different countries over the years, including: Armenia, Russia, Ukraine, Sri Lanka, Philippines, Panama, Peru, Guatemala, and Canada (Parry Sound).

We need to have a reason for getting up in the morning. Thinking that every day for the rest of your life you are going to be sitting around doing absolutely nothing is very scary. I still, to this day, get cabin fever if I sit in the apartment too long. In the old days, when you retired, you *did* retire. My father and my wife's father just sat down and rocked in their chairs. Their life span after retirement wasn't very long but I believe it could have been longer if they went on doing something.

I am a huge believer in the fact that if you don't physically work your body and mentally work your mind, they deteriorate very fast. I believe our body and mind need to have some stress to stay healthy.

When I first retired, I wondered if that was all that there was. I thought I was done now, that was it! Volunteering for something like CESO filled all those needs for me. I felt I still had something to offer and got the satisfaction of really helping people. It fills your social needs. That's another thing you lose when you stop working, your world shrinks very quickly.

I really wanted to travel, but could only afford to do so much travelling. CESO filled that need as well, in a different way. It's very different, working in those places, rather than being a tourist there. It broadened my horizons.

Your job is who you are, like it or not, and when you retire, you lose the status that comes with it. You should never underestimate the importance your social needs and status needs.

I have 12 grandchildren. Family, to me, is extremely important. I feel sorry for those who don't have it, it's not a given. Some people, for all kind of reasons, don't have family, just knowing they are there and supporting you and caring for you. I was blessed with four great sons who have married four great ladies. I now have a wonderful group of grandkids. Part of aging is sometimes getting sick. When I was in hospital, some of my grandkids would come in and care for me and clean up after me. They have been a great part of my retirement years.

CESO, family, walking, and my marriage have all been a big part of my retirement years. I have been married for one hell of a long time. We have had each other and been able to support each other through illnesses. That's been really important. We do it back and forth.

There wasn't much of an adjustment period in our marriage when I retired before my wife, because I gradually wound down my work, it didn't just stop. I gradually began filling in the void with volunteering. You can get depressed quite easily if you are not careful, you have to fight it. I have never gone into a deep depression but I have periods when I feel depressed and think I am just waiting here for whatever they choose to throw at me, and I die. That is not an uplifting thought. If you sit in your chair and think about it too much, it can take over and your health deteriorates. As a result, I keep very busy with my volunteer work at CESO.

Probably, on average, I work a day or two a week volunteering at CESO, where I am involved in a variety of activities including: orientation sessions, interviewing candidates, volunteer representative on the Appeals Committee, working with Lead Volunteers and mentoring students.

My Advice

- Doing nothing except taking vacations and playing golf all the time should not be an option.

- Do not be in a hurry to retire if you are still productive and enjoying work.
- If you can wind down slowly, it is better to gradually retire.
- In many ways, lots of us are defined by our work and we shouldn't ignore it nor the importance of the social aspects of work.
- When you retire, it is important to think about what you enjoy doing the most in your job. Then you should look and see how you can use your expertise and years of experience.
- Define what "turns you on" and look for ways to use your skills and experience in other retirement activities.

Name:	Dorothy S.
Occupation:	Medical Radiation Technologist
Retirement Age:	69
Current Age:	71
Protirement Activities:	**Community Builder; Hobbyist;** Travel Enthusiast

My Protirement Story

When I retired it was June and I thought, "You know what, I need a rest; I need to unwind from this whole life and turmoil, so I'm taking the summer off." I had some trilogy books that I wanted to read, and I wanted to get back to my golfing. But I think it's more important what I didn't do. I did not de-clutter my house; I did not rearrange my cupboards. I chilled the whole summer; I played some golf and went on a couple of weekend trips with friends. I hosted some barbecues at my house for some of my neighbours and was there for my daughter and her two children.

Then winter came. I don't think it was depression but I was moody and unmotivated. I didn't want to go out, all that kind of stuff. That's when I cleaned my cupboards. But one of the things that my late husband had asked me to do was to think about volunteering at the Carpenter Hospice. In 2007 he died at the

Carpenter Hospice and before dying he spoke to me about volunteering there. I never got around to volunteering.

I joined Rotary and knew right away that's what I wanted to do; give back through Rotary. That was one of the best things I ever did. The friends I made there, the support that I received, was unbelievable. This year I decided to volunteer at the Hospice.

I'm saving my money to plan different trips. I want to go to Normandy and Vimy Ridge; go on a river cruise, and go dog-sledding.

My Advice

- Take your time in transitioning.
- Don't jump into activities.
- Do things for you, things you enjoy, things that you may have been putting off.
- Find a new identity, a new purpose in life. This may take a while on where you are in your life. No need to rush.
- Have a plan and don't feel guilty if all you want to do is relax and read a book, you are tired!

Name: Graham Kennedy
Occupation: Presbyterian Minister
Retirement Age: 65
Current Age: 69
Protirement Activities: **Community Builder,** Hobbyist, Health Enthusiast; Family Enthusiast

My Protirement Story

The presbytery decided that a minister who retires should not go back to his own church for four years. So, I have not gone back to Knox. I don't know when I would go back, even to attend services. It's tough stuff, after 18 years, suddenly all my connections with daily life are cut off. I now attend Stamford Church in Niagara

Falls. It's not quite like 'home' (which has gone away), but the minster is outstanding.

So, when I came to retirement, and when I took away all that fabric of my daily activity, in some ways, I came to the edge of a cliff. You can say, “Okay, I don’t know that I have a parachute; I’m not sure what I’m supposed to do now.” I did that once on a ski hill. I was just learning how to ski and I looked down this ski hill and thought, “Oh my, that’s too scary; I think I’ll take the alternate route,” which was on my right. I looked and the alternate route on the right was a precipice. So, you either go down a precipice or you go down the hill. I went back and forth in my mind about which way should I go. I didn’t have any problem going down the hill, once I said, “No, no, no, there’s a way I am going over the precipice.”

I have been a Rotary member for a number of years. The paradox is that, in the church, you try to convince people to put their faith into action. In Rotary, the people are doing everything that I wanted them to do in the church.

I think there was a gap now. My routine used to be going to the church in the morning, coming home at noon for lunch, and sometimes having a swim before going back to work. I still swim during the noon hour; that’s continuity. I have kept that routine. Golfing is Wednesday morning, which I was not doing, obviously, when I was working.

Deep down, I think I am being given orders and will continue to be given orders, from above. I basically say “yes” to almost everything I’m asked to do. Someone calls me up and says, “I need someone to preach on August 28th,” I say, “Put me down.” It is the same with Rotary. Rotary always says, “If you’re asked, say yes.” I haven’t said no yet. I don’t have any trouble filling the time, although it’s…sometimes, it’s a challenge. My wife is still working. When she quits or retires, which is very soon, I’ll have someone to tell me what to do.

I find that the body’s not as co-operative as it used to be. I have had trouble at times sleeping because my leg hurts. It may be arthritis, since my mother had arthritis. I have had prostate cancer.

I garden; in the morning, I water the plants. I could spend time in that garden all day, if I want to. I take my swim from 11:30–12:00. When I have time, I support my kids. Today, I am helping one of my daughters buy a car. We have three cats, so it's always work around here. You learn to fill the time.

I do Sudoku puzzles for fun. I have played chess and bridge all my life but haven't played lately. My wife brings home a reading list in the summertime and we read through the books. We also watch TV regularly.

My Advice

- Have some interests during your working life that you can continue with after retirement.
- Be an involved volunteer before retirement so you can continue after retirement.
- Accept retirement as a part of life and go with it.

Name:	Rosemary D. H.
Occupation:	Educator, Dean, Faculty of Humanities
Retirement Age:	72
Current Age:	73
Protirement Activities:	**Community Builder;** Writer

My Protirement Story

I don't really believe in this word, "retirement." I had a lot of trouble as the date approached because I really loved what I was doing. The last few years of my job as Dean were largely focused on opening up a new School of Fine and Performing Arts, working with the city on the Performing Arts Centre and seeing the Faculty of Humanities flourish. All very exciting.

The Marilyn I Walker School of Fine and Performing Arts would open just as I was getting ready to retire. I went to the ground breaking and found myself weeping, tears of both joy and a sense of loss. Fortunately, my partner was wonderful. What did I do for self-care? I got a really good therapist and began to understand the transition that I was in. It led me to volunteer at Hospice Niagara. It is as soul-satisfying as teaching, only now I'm the learner.

I have always loved books! I had a huge library at home and huge library at the office. The office had to be emptied and completely spotless by June 30th. I ended up keeping a great many of them, but I gladly donated nearly a third of my library to a book sale benefitting student scholarships in philosophy. I don't know what shedding a snake skin would be like, but I think it might be something like this.

The transition experience is hard to describe. I know that I loved being a leader, in charge and directing. But, that is what I love *not* doing now. Now, I love being part of a team, and not the head of something. I love the fact that what I do is really shared.

I am a board member with the Foster Festival, but after my term ends in August, I know that I will never sit on another board. My life from now on has to do with not directing people and projects. This is really consistent with my volunteer experience at Hospice Niagara. I love it and feel so privileged. I work on creating Legacy Projects for the Day Hospice guests and also co-facilitate Grief Circles. It's an honour, being beside someone for such a significant journey. So, that's what's going on in my little river of life now. I get so much back; it is amazing.

It's also fostering my writing. I'm about half way through my first book, a piece of historical fiction. It's called *God's Tokens* and is about the plague ravaging a small town in 14th century Germany and the horrific blame placed on the Jews as scapegoats. And, after finishing this book, I have another that is starting to take form and it's about the nature of body and soul and grows out of years of teaching comparative religion.

I once read that we need spiritual, political, and creative experiences to be fully satisfied. I feel, for the first time in my life, these are in balance.

My Advice

- Dispense with the word "Congratulations" when people speak to someone who has just retired. For example, "Oh you're retiring, congratulations!" It should be thought of as another chapter, maybe saying something like, "How exciting!"
- Follow your passions.
- Take some risks.

- Have an adventure.
- You are turning the pages of this chapter; you're the author.
- In the Hospice training, they say that people die the way they live. Maybe people also retire the way they live.

Name: Sandra H.
Occupation: Military Management
Retirement Age: 50
Current Age: 55
Protirement Activities: **Community Builder;** New Career/Job; Travel Enthusiast; Life Long Leaner; Family Enthusiast

My Protirement Story

I'm a spiritual person and I've always felt that God was guiding my hand as to where I was and what I was doing. I had faith that God would lead me to the next thing. He said, "Be still and know that all will be revealed in My time." It was a very calming for me. I gave up my job and knew that I was to go to South America. I ended up living in Peru for five months, working with children; helping teenagers with their English homework and playing games with the younger kids and providing medical care assisting an American Pediatrician. Since then, I have been involved with another community organization, called CCAMRE, which is: Canadian–Central American Relief Effort. This organization has many programs including medical and dental care, education programs and community building projects in the Merendon Mountains of Guatemala.

I am also actively involved with Rotary working on several committees. My mother is 82 and has breast cancer. She's gone through cancer treatment but she's presently fairly healthy. I'm now living with her as my father died 11 years ago. Both of my adult sons now live out West. They're both working in the gas and oil industry.

I miss my military colleagues because they're a lot of great people, but Facebook is good that way. I've stayed in touch with friends all over the world. After I had come back to Canada I moved back here to St. Catharines. I am now working part-time for a chiropractor as a receptionist. When you talk about status, it's funny how there are some people who judge you because they see you sitting behind a desk being a receptionist. I really like the job, though, and there are wonderful people that come into the office and don't judge me.

I'm active in my church. I'm in charge of the women's ministry, active in Bible Study Fellowship and a member of the "United Federation of University Women."

I'll be going back to school. I love to learn. I've already gone back to the college to do bread-baking and to do things that I enjoy. I enjoy taking lots of different cooking courses. I've been thinking about going back and doing another CPR course. I also love to travel to find out about different cultures.

I see myself moving west, once my kids start getting married and having kids, and probably once my mum passes on.

My Advice

- It's really, really important to have outside activities, to have hobbies.
- Give back.
- Continue to learn, keep your mind active.
- Find your passion.

Community Builder: Planning & Advocacy

Name:	Diana E.
Occupation:	Consultant, Community Organizer
Retirement Age:	68
Current Age:	70
Protirement Activities:	**Community Builder**

My Protirement Story

At the time my 35 years of consulting work life was ending, my long, wonderful and challenging relationship was also coming to a close. Indeed, a time of leavings—a time of loose ends! I had to decide what I was going to do with the rest of my life in all those circumstances.

I was on the centenary committee for my church, which was turning a hundred years old here in Vancouver. We invited David Suzuki to come and speak on Environment and the Economy. He talked about environment issues and the need for attitude change and action. His words really resonated with me. I went home thinking, "Well, maybe I'm hearing a 'call,' maybe something's going on here." I started to read a whole lot of the environment books. I went to a couple of introductory sessions at various environment groups. Nothing quite fit, but I kept moseying about. Then, a friend handed me a little advertising postcard saying, "Suzuki Elders Environment Forum, November 2009." I attended the forum, loved it, and wrote reams on the evaluation form. I got a call, saying, "Will you come to a meeting? We're trying to get more people involved, and we're trying to do some re-organizing." I started going to some of the meetings of the Suzuki Elder Council, and found a place for myself there, not the least of which was helping them to develop a mission statement.

I've been the Chair of the Elder Council for three years now. Being involved with the Suzuki Elders fell into step with all my skills, but it was also a new field of interest, a new community of interesting people, and a cause close to my heart.

This is a wonderful group to be involved with. Working and volunteering with them has helped me rethink a word I have never liked: "retire!" Instead, I think of this time as an opportunity to *re-tire*, like putting new tires on a vehicle that still works well.

My Advice

On entering this new phase of life, I now realize that I considered interests of both heart and mind. Here they are, much more formulated now than then!

- What is my life story so far? What's missing? Where are the gaps? Do I want to put my heart and mind to filling some of those gaps?
- What do I want to learn more about? A new field entirely? Another angle on something familiar?

- Where can I best be of use in the world in this phase of my life? Family? Community? Issues? Myself? What difference can I (any of us!) make and where? What skills do I bring, what skills can I learn?

Name:	Domenic V.
Occupation:	Director of Senior Services, Regional Government
Retirement Age:	60
Current Age:	65
Protirement Activities:	**Community Builder;** Caregiver; Hobbyist; Health Enthusiast; Family Enthusiast

My Protirement Story

I was chairing an Age-Friendly Community Committee when I retired. They said to me, “You aren’t going to retire from this Committee, are you?” I told them that I was given advice from some people who had retired not to make any commitments after I retired for the first six months. So, here I was, breaking the rule one week into my six months. I said yes I would chair it but only if I could get a co-chair. So, they found a co-chair and I continued with the committee.

The transition into retirement was largely positive for me. It gave me some time to reflect on where I was going with my life. Initially, I treated it like an extended vacation but it felt different, with less pressure, because with my other vacations I always knew I was returning to a backlog of work.

My wife had retired before me and had expectations on what it might mean; probably about me catching up with my domestic chores which were always backlogged because of my work pressures. I told her it wasn’t me to just sit around. We had some discussions about how we were going to spend our joint retirement years. She knew me and knew that I wasn’t going to linger about the house.

We did lots of biking and some travel that first summer. I also had a grandson the previous October and that was the catalyst for me to rethink my priorities. He was born with a heart defect and within four days had major heart surgery. I could have retired a couple of years earlier and that experience helped me think about my priorities. He's now going to be five and is healthy.

Knowing that our muscles lose mass and can atrophy as we age, I joined a gym after I retired. That also enabled me to continue my tennis over the winter because my gym has indoor tennis courts. I like hanging out with my wife in the morning and reading the newspaper. I was also recruited to be a volunteer at Linhaven Long-term Care Home with fund raising and working in their garden.

I became more involved as a volunteer with the Age-Friendly Community Committee. I was also asked to apply for a volunteer board member position with the Local Health Integration Network and was accepted. I have an aging 90-year-old mother who is a widow and still living at home. She is wonderful and mentally sharp but that still takes up a bit of my time. We now have a second grandchild in Toronto. We usually go their weekly and prepare dinner. I enjoy cooking and made a resolution that I would learn at least one new recipe each week in my retired years.

I have more time with family and I also have more time to spend with my tennis and hockey friends.

My Advice

- Think through your priorities, your passions in life and expand on them when you retire.
- Leave room for new activities, for growth, for new discoveries.
- Have leisure activities.
- Allow for spontaneity.
- Include time for health, exercise and diet.

Name: Helen C.
Occupation: Town Clerk; Not-for Profit Sector Manager
Retirement Age: 64
Current Age: 66
Protirement Activities: **Community Builder**; New Career/Job

My Protirement Story

I've always belonged to the Chamber of Commerce regardless of the community I lived in. The same was true during my 13-year career in Sarnia Lambton. Within a year of moving to Sarnia Lambton, I was on the Board. I did my three-year stint on the Sarnia Chamber Board. I then joined the Board of Directors for our local hospital and did that for another three years.

The very first thing I did when I retired was join the Sarnia Chamber of Commerce. My last job was very stressful, leaving me close to a nervous breakdown. So, for about six months after I retired, I did nothing. I continued volunteer work that I was involved in. Then, I had a knee replacement; that's not a fun thing to do. It took up about a year and a half to recover. And then I started thinking, "I want to do something." So, I started doing some small facilitation work.

I really believe that if you just quit your job and stay home, you're not going to live long. I have been doing some really fun volunteer work since I retired. As a volunteer and as paid staff, I organized a lobby trip to Queen's Park with a reception for the MPP's. The Queen's Park reception showcased all the local food produced by the farmers in Lambton County. In addition to other fundraiser events, I organized "BarnBQ" for the Ontario Sugar Beet Growers and was welcomed into the farming community. I am now a patient experience volunteer at Bluewater Health. There's a group of us who are the "voice of the patients" and we're becoming well-recognized within the hospital. Staff are looking for "PEVs," to sit on their various committees to provide "the voice of the patients." I also chair the local Tourism Sarnia-Lambton (at the time of publishing, I am past chair).

Currently, I am working for Goodwill by providing assistance as they move into different areas of funding by assisting them in the creation of a Fund Development Plan for the organization.

My Advice

- You need to be thinking about what's important to you; what would give meaning to your life.
- It's important that you understand what makes you tick, because it's unhealthy to just sit home when you retire.
- Do things you love doing.
- Be open to new opportunities. When one door closes, another opens.
- Embrace life and all it offers!

CHAPTER 15: PROTIREMENT CATEGORY #11: SOCIALIZERS

"I'm definitely a people person.
I love socializing and being around people,
and having a good conversation."
Emily Deschanel

Introduction

Today, when you mention social networking, the first thing people think about is social media, networking online. Baby Boomers grew up with a different understanding of social networking, one that involved face-to-face contact. Everyone has social networks that include friends and family. Some Baby Boomers really enjoy developing social networks to enhance their lives and those of their friends. I call this Protirement Category, "Socializers."

Facts about Socializers

Socializers are engaged in a process where they bring together friends with similar interests in formal and informal groups. The focus of these groups is often around friendship, a common interest, providing support to group members, intellectual stimulation, and providing a feeling of community.

Socializers are organizers and facilitators of social groups and enjoy joining other groups as well. They are very aware of the benefits of socializing in groups, such as: an increase in feelings of inclusion and happiness, an increase in quality of life for the group members, and a reduction in isolation and improvement of brain functioning.

Alex Brain wrote in the *Just Breathe* website that there are nine important benefits of real-time face-to-face socializing versus online socializing.[26] They include:

- "Helping in building positive and constructive relationships via the real social networks that are formed;
- Socializing plays a pivotal role in improving overall growth and development of an individual;
- Socializing enhances mental functioning, as the mind is kept occupied with real thoughts;
- Stress and anxiety levels can be reduced to a great extent. Solutions to problems may be found in dialogue with group members;
- It provides great opportunity to understand various kinds of people, their mannerisms, personalities, thought processes, and so on. Socializing develops better understanding of human perspectives and attributes;
- Socializing is a great tool for development of self-confidence and giving your self-esteem the required boost. It kicks out shyness and hesitance from an individual, making them ready to face the world in a smart manner;
- It produces happiness and joy when you meet your friends and family in real rather than online life, as you can share issues and emotions more explicitly;
- Socializing is a great way of giving and getting emotional, physical, and spiritual support. Even if you are feeling down and upset with something, friends and family can help you overcome the difficult period with ease. They can cheer you up, provide the required encouragement, and bring back your lost zeal and enthusiasm."

Social media, emails, video calls, etc., are all excellent modes of communicating and staying in touch with friends and family, but they lack the human contact that personal groups provide, and this is what Socializers create for their friends; an opportunity to have regular face-to-face interaction and social contact.

"Socializers" Protirement Stories

Two people interviewed were active Socializers. They were 71 and 75 years old.

"Socializers" personal Protirement Stories follow.

Name:	Jeanette L.
Occupation:	Non-Profit Executive
Retirement Age:	65
Current Age:	71
Protirement Activities:	**Socializer;** Writer; Health Enthusiast; Family Enthusiast

My Protirement Story

I always planned to work until I was 65. About three weeks before my retirement date, I was told that I needed hip surgery. I retired, went on a waiting list and had hip surgery six months later. The surgery forced me to sit in my chair and think about post-retirement life.

A few months before I retired, I heard a CBC interview with Andy Barrie, former Metro Morning host. He talked about staying cognitively active after retirement and focusing on brain outputs. This interview sparked an interest in writing. I started writing a blog a few months before I retired as a strategy to maintain cognitive fitness!

Life changed quickly after retirement. I had a large send-off event with about 400 people from my professional network attending, many of whom I didn't really know. I stay in touch with some of those people but they were work associates, not close friends. I was tired after I retired and happy that emails stopped coming. I enjoyed a leisure break; I can't say that I really missed my career.

Since 1984, we have cottaged at Lake Huron where we have a number of friends. I started to socialize more with the 'lake' people. As well, I joined a book club at the public library. Through that book club, I met several women who are dear friends now. We play bridge together, socialize, and travel together. I joined two of them on a six week tour of South Africa last year.

It's surprising how new friendships and different networks develop after 'work' ends. Meeting new people happens easily when there is time for varied activities. For example, after I retired, I had more time at the gym. I didn't just rush into the gym after work and rush away to get home. Aqua fit classes helped with rehabilitation after surgery. At my gym, there is a lovely restaurant and bar, which is a great meeting place for coffee or lunch after swimming or other workouts. Now I have my gym friends, my book club friends, and my bridge friends.

After I retired, I made the mistake of accepting far too many volunteer board commitments. One lovely summer day, I was sitting in a boardroom. As I gazed out the window I wondered "Why am I doing this – this is another four-hour meeting in a stuffy board room with uncomfortable chairs – I've already spent my career life in stuffy board rooms." I decided not to continue with volunteer boards and change course. I resigned from all of those boards and committees to free up time for fun.

The tag line for my postworksavvy.com blog (www.postworksavvy.com) is "Inspirations for successful retirement." I write about the non-financial aspects of retirement that people struggle with; how they deal spend their time; how they live their lives; how they relate to their adult children; how they deal with grandchildren; and various things that people who are retired think about, talk about, worry about. About 52% of my subscribers are Canadian, 30% are American, with the remainder from Australia, New Zealand, and Britain. I have just over 200 subscribers now, and well over a 200 hits a day.

My husband of 50 years is 80 now; his health has been failing in the past few months. He retired at 65 when it was compulsory but then worked on part-time teaching and counseling contracts at a community college up to age 77. Until a month ago, we lived in a too-big house in Markham and did all the gardening ourselves. We are in the process of moving to London to be closer to my son and daughter-in-law and also closer to our cottage.

Around the time I retired, one of my friends told me that it is probably better that two partners don't retire at the same time, and I think he was right about that. Once my husband retired, I was already into my retirement routine so he was able to develop his own routine separate from mine.

My Advice

- You need a plan but it shouldn't be too rigid – allow for serendipity.
- Eat nutritiously, exercise, develop social relationships, and avoid isolation.
- Stay open to new ideas, new experiences, take a few risks.
- Protect your relationship with your partner.

Name:	Joanne T.
Occupation:	Teacher, Community Planner, Child Advocate
Retirement Age:	58
Current Age:	75
Protirement Activities:	**Socializer;** Community Builder; Family Enthusiast

My Protirement Story

I retired in 1999 when I was 58. I returned to St. Catharines and my first year was spent getting to know St. Catharines again. I did some contract work with the District Health Council, joined a feminist choir and, in a couple of years began curling, which I had never done before.

I added things incrementally. There was a group called Niagara Pride that I got involved with. It was a small group of volunteers who were concerned about kids who were lesbian and gay. We hadn't heard about transgendered at that time. We began a monthly drop-in program at the library for kids so they could tell their parents that they were going to the library, if they weren't "out."

When the idea of a new community health center (CHC) in Niagara came along, I jumped on the band wagon. I was really keen because I knew that it would make a really good fit. By that time, I knew something about trans individuals, and they had absolutely no help in St. Catharines. I knew that a lot of gay and lesbian people were underserved in regards to their health needs, as well.

In 2004, I started volunteering on the planning committee and then the founding board, eventually becoming Chair. I loved the notion of delivering health services in a very holistic health focused way rather than an illness focused way. As soon as I got off the board at Quest CHC, I got onto the board of PFLAG, Parents and Friends of Lesbians and Gays. I have been volunteering with them ever since.

I am still singing with the choir and enjoying it. Also, for a very long time, since I came back to St. Catharines, I have been chairing the local RPAC, the Residential Placement Advisory Committee, which is a committee that reviews kids who are in residential placement of 10 beds or more. It's a provincially legislated function.

I belong to a group of women who meet once in a while but used to meet monthly. Everybody is retired and spending winters in Mexico and God knows where. We call ourselves Sister Crones. It was an interesting group when it began because, other than me, everybody had sons. They were feminists who had sons. They were interested in things about aging. It is a discussion/support group of about 10 women. We were all in our middle 50s. We are still meeting, but much less formally.

I also belong to another group of women who meet as a salon. It is another conversation group but the conversation can be much broader. This is an amazing group of women. We haven't been going for very long, maybe a year and a half.

I brought a group of women together who are all lesbian, and some of whom were lesbian orphans, they were here but didn't know anybody else. We get together every single week, we go to a pub for dinner, and celebrate each other's birthdays.

For the past year and a bit, I have been seeing a woman in Hamilton who has three absolutely delightful grandchildren. They are so much fun but exhausting. She has a cottage, so there is also time at the cottage.

There's another group of four women who get together every two weeks. We do some crafts together. Everybody does their own thing. I also do travelling art with this group and with a friend in Montreal. Travelling art is a project that somebody begins, and then you add to it, and then it is passed on. It is really fun, you never know how it is going to evolve.

I don't have much time for more. It's the right amount of busy, though. I also like to read, watch TV sometimes, putter about in my garden, and try to keep my house in some relative form of order.

I own this house with another woman. We have divided the house up and down so I have the upstairs and she has the downstairs. She looks after the backyard and I look after the front yard. We have a backyard and every afternoon at 4:00 pm there may be people here who have a drink together. We call it "foursies." It is from four to five o'clock and then everyone goes home. People drop in. There are several people who could show up on any given day.

My life feels quite balanced. I am quite social. I have friends I spend time with every week, who are really important to me. My kids are far away, in Vancouver and Mexico, so I visit and they visit.

My Advice

- If you're happy in your work, keep at it.
- Just do it, retire and enjoy.
- Friends are very important.
- Being able to be creative is important.
- Give back to the community.

CHAPTER 16: PROTIREMENT CATEGORY #12: WRITERS & PERFORMERS

"I love words. I love to sing them and to speak them and even now, I must admit, I have fallen into the joy of writing them."
Anne Rice

Introduction

Many people have a dream of writing books, poetry, and music, as well as performing when they retire, but only some follow through on those dreams. I was fortunate to interview poets, authors, musicians, and a community theatre actor. They all thoroughly love the creative outlet they have developed in their Protirement.

Facts about Writers & Performers

Boomers are embracing the arts more than ever before. We are becoming authors of fiction and non-fiction books; we are writing articles for magazines, local newspapers, and publishing our own blogs. Boomers are returning to their roots and writing poetry and music. Others are performing in community theatre, coffee houses, and clubs. Along with the rapid development of the internet, anyone can self-publish their books and music. Social media provides individuals with a vehicle for writing and music. The internet has expanded the creative world for Boomers.

"Writers and Performers" Protirement Stories

I interviewed five people who were involved in writing and performing as their primary Protirement activity. They ranged in age from 64 to 78. Two individuals wrote poetry while one was also a lyricist and performer. One person wrote fiction novels, one wrote non-fiction while the third wrote both fiction and non-fiction novels.

"Writers/Performers" personal Protirement Stories follow.

Name:	Anna Porter
Occupation:	Publisher, Author
Retirement Age:	NA
Current Age:	NA
Protirement Activities:	**Writer**

My Protirement Story

My career as a publisher was exciting and fun, and I loved it. I sold my interest in Key Porter Books in 2004 to focus on writing. While I was still publishing books, I started writing novels and wrote three mysteries. The last of them was a book called *The Book Fair Murders*, which was made into a TV film.

I then started to write something closer to the bone, a book called *The Storyteller*. It was about my Hungarian roots and my grandfather who was a magical presence in my early life. He is the storyteller in *The Storyteller. The Storyteller* came out when I was still publishing. Then I became very involved in researching and writing a book about the Holocaust in Hungary. In the course of researching and interviewing Holocaust survivors, I really discovered that it was vastly more engaging and required more time than my career as a book publisher. I was less able to hide it in the cracks of my publishing career. It contributed to my wanting to get out of the business. We sold our shares in the business in 2004, and I stayed on for about a year and then I quit.

I have been writing full time since then. I miss my friends in the business, I miss the excitement of publishing something new. One of the aspects of the business that I was quite good at was coming up with book ideas and then matching them to people. I can't help watching the news and saying, oh my God, there's a book! One of the last books I worked on was Norman Jewison's autobiography. He's an amazing filmmaker, one of the best in the world. That was a privilege and was fun. The title of that book is: *This Terrible Business That Has Been Good to Me*.

I finished the Hungarian Holocaust book. It's called: *Kasztner's Train*. I went on to write a book about Eastern Europe joining the rest of Europe, called: *The Ghosts of Europe*. It is still fairly current as there is still a lot of debate between east and west Europe. It is not as united as we think. These books won a couple of awards, which is really encouraging for a writer, knowing that you are appreciated.

I have finished a novel, called *The Appraisal,* which will be published in September 2017. I am reaching a second draft of my memoir about working in the book business, which will be published next fall. Writing is not easy and I don't consider it a retirement activity, but it is enormously satisfying.

My Advice

- Stay engaged with what is happening around you in the world.
- Keep your social conscience.
- Don't become a golfer to the exclusion of social issues.

Name:	Linda F.
Occupation:	Sociologist Professor, Poet
Retirement Age:	63
Current Age:	64
Protirement Activities:	**Writer;** Health Enthusiast

My Protirement Story

The first thing I had to do was learn to cook. My husband had been the main cook at home and he asked me to begin preparing dinners since I retired first.

I swim three times a week at a rec centre, and work on my poetry writing almost every day.

At work, my office was a social hub for students and colleagues. Colleagues still keep in touch but I don't miss the activity at the office very much. Unfortunately, the work environment had changed a lot, and more and more teaching was shifting to online. It had become more tiring to grade papers, student work quality and writing skills had decreased, so it was time to leave, to retire.

The first year went by quickly. I am in the second year and I finished my fourth book of poetry due out in the spring. Right now I am well into my fifth, while also trying to write a novel.

I can now write when I want to, I do not have to do it on the weekends, which is when I did it when I was working. It's more like when I was a grad student and writing my thesis.

My days are flexible, though I keep somewhat structured. I read a lot more. The only things that really regulate my day are swimming when the pool is open, and having dinner prepared for 6:30 p.m.

I am now able to spend more time at the cottage with my husband and feel less of a need to write all summer. Retirement gives me more time to spend with my husband.

My Advice

- I have no advice for my kids. They will sort retirement life out for themselves.

Name: Max Layton
Occupation: Teacher
Retirement Age: 65
Current Age: 71
Protirement Activities: **Writer/Performer**

My Protirement Story

I retired when I was 65. If someone had said, "Okay, Mr. Layton, you're a really good teacher; we'd like you to come in and teach one class, part-time." or alternatively, "Come in two days a week," I would have happily done it. It would've gotten me up every morning. Unfortunately, union rules prevent this.

I'm a voracious reader, I love reading. I love discussing ideas and I'm a very, very argumentative discusser. I like a good argument. I also love cross-country skiing and canoe-tripping.

I learned to play guitar when I was a child. Leonard Cohen, a friend of my father, taught me how to play the guitar. I love writing poetry and songs. Every month, I go to a place in Toronto called the Tranzac Club. I'm the co-host of a gig there. It's a coffeehouse, except they sell beer. It's in the Annex area and has been around since the 60s. Once a month, my co-host, Robert Priest, who is also a poet and an incredible songwriter, and I host a two-hour gig, every second Sunday of every month. We always have a special guest. It has become very popular, not only with the growing audience but also with other musicians and songwriters in Toronto. Right now we are booked more than six months in advance; we're booked solid. I get e-mails, "Do you have a place for me?" "Well, I'm sorry, but the nearest I can talk about is maybe next year."

The point I'm really trying to make is, I get the same pleasure from walking into the Tranzac and starting my set as I did teaching. I always do a set, Robert does a set, and then the special guest does a set. Nothing but music and poetry for two hours! I so look forward to this every month that it spurs me on.

I don't think there's been a single month that's gone by, in the last two years, when I didn't have a new song ready for the audience in the Tranzac. I've just got to have a song. And oddly enough, something happens. There have been times when it's two days before the show and I don't have anything. And then, just suddenly, bingo, it comes. This August will be the first time that I'm not going to be there, because I'm going to Cape Breton in order to finish my latest book of poems.

These last five years, since my retirement from teaching, have been tremendously liberating. For the first time in my life, I have financial security. I'm debt-free and I own this home. That's a river right down there, the Credit River. I can swim in it, and I do practically every day. And in the winter, I skate on it. This is all woods all around us, with a beautiful trail, the Bruce Trail. I go cross-country skiing. So, I am healthy. I'm not wealthy, but I'm secure. And this has given me the freedom to release three CDs of my songs and publish three books of poetry. Finally, I have some stability, and a really good woman who is my wife, and we are very happy. So, that's the end of my story.

My Advice

- Be honest about your own heart.
- Do something that really matters to you.

Name:	Michael C.
Occupation:	Reporter
Retirement Age:	57
Current Age:	69
Protirement Activities:	**Writer**

My Protirement Story

I retired in 2005 but I remained quite busy. I had quite a lot of interest in my projects. The Glenn Gould book that I wrote became a documentary. I was going to have my own TV show called Danger Man, on CBC. At that time, I was called the "fear doctor" because I had these books on fear. Unfortunately it didn't get off the ground.

We moved to Fort Erie in 2010. I started suffering from depression because things slowed down. I was doing some free lance writing for media, but it slowed down as the print media industry slowed down. Book publishing started to really hurt. I went through a dry period from 2010, when my Poltergeist book was published, until today with my new book on the Daredevils of Niagara Falls. I did some free lancing for the Life Section of the Toronto Star over that time, and I have done some professional speaking on fear and stress.

I have a lot of determination which in the end seems to carry me through the depression. My emotional drive carries me through the hard times along with my support network which is very good. My wife understands me and is very supportive along with my family. We are coming into a golden age of mental health awareness and we are in a good place. People are finally talking about it today.

I am physically active and still play basketball and soccer. I also coach soccer teams. I was just inducted in to Niagara Christian College Sports Hall of Fame.

It's physically impossible for me to slow down. I can't ever retire. It's just not part of me. I just go from one project to another. I miss working for newspapers. I get depressed when I get bored. My wife once said that I don't fear anything but I do fear boredom.

My Advice

- Love and be loved.
- Chose activities in retirement that you love doing.
- Lean on one another, have a support system.

Name:	Robert D.
Occupation:	Social Worker, Professor
Retirement Age:	66
Current Age:	78
Protirement Activities:	**Writer;** Socializer

My Protirement Story

In 2005, after a very serious car accident, I was forced to give up my full-time contract to teach and help organize a post graduate social development degree in Thailand. Along with rehab, I retired. At 66, I began writing my first book. Interspersed with my writing, I returned to Thailand three times to teach, one year at a time. On two occasions, I taught and advised postgraduate students at Naresuan University, in lower northern Thailand. My second trip was at a university in Chiang Rai, in the Golden Triangle where I taught, advised, and became the founding editor of a new journal of social development in the Mekong Region.

I published my first book, *The Tangerine Murders: Dancing with Death*, in 2012. I am now releasing my second book, entitled, "*Ghosts in the Brothel*."

For me, imagination has always been a big part of my life. I have always read a lot and written professional articles, books, and reports, as well as poetry. Writing has, you might say, been in my blood. Writing mystery books has been on my bucket list.

My own peer group is getting older, that's the reality. However, I have friends of all ages here and in other places, where I have lived—Vietnam, Thailand, and Australia. With my writing as well as with social media, it is easier today to stay in contact with family and friends in my networks.

My Advice

- Be yourself.
- Life is precarious, fragile, live it in the moment.
- Don't just lose people in your network, keep in touch.
- Find interests that keep your mind and body active.

CHAPTER 17: PROTIREMENT CATEGORY #13: HEALTH ENTHUSIASTS

"Health is like money. We never have a true idea of its value until we lose it."
Josh Billings

Introduction

Baby Boomers will live longer than any previous generation. Boomers have grown up with variety of health promotion programs. During our lifetime, smoking has become unacceptable in most circles and is banned from public spaces; driving with seatbelts has become a norm; regular exercising, gym memberships, yoga, martial arts, jogging, walking, tennis, and many other forms of exercise have become mainstream activities for Boomers. A growing awareness of healthy nutrition is found all around us, on social media, TV, radio, and in newspapers, and fast food restaurants are working overtime to create healthier food options.

We incorporate these messages in different ways. Some of us are healthier than others. There is a group of Boomers who have focused their primary Protirement activities on health. I consider this group the Health Enthusiasts.

Facts about Health Enthusiasts

Boomers are the first generation to be targeted by government led health promotion programs and health advertisers. It is not surprising that we take our health seriously. Previous generations have slowed down as they have aged, believing that the body should have less physical activity the older we got. Our generation now knows that slowing down our physical activity actually speeds up the aging process. Our muscles need regular activity to remain healthy.

While not all Boomers have taken heed of this knowledge, there is a group of Boomers who are Health Enthusiasts and enjoy focusing on their health as a primary Protirement activity. They are involved in regular physical exercise, mental wellness activities, and healthy nutrition.

"Health Enthusiasts" Protirement Stories

I interviewed two individuals who were Health Enthusiasts. They were 75 and 79 years old.

"Health Enthusiasts" personal Protirement Stories follow.

Name: Brian D.
Occupation: Business Owner, Model
Retirement Age: 67
Current Age: 79
Protirement Activities: **Health Enthusiast**; Hobbyist; Community Builder

My Protirement Story

When I retired, not much changed. I stopped working in my business but continued to do some modeling, competitive running, and working out every day. I also play tennis and took up golf.

I had a couple of injuries, which made me realize that I should stop doing marathons, of which I had done 57. I still try to break a sweat every day. Cycling has been a savior and easier on the body than running. My wife is seventeen years younger, also works out every day, and still works in her own business, which adds some interest to our lives. We are active in her Rotary Club. We cycle, golf, and ski together, and love to travel. Our common love of sports and fine wine keeps life fun.

My retirement was pretty seamless. Staying fit helped fill the void. Social life is important too, especially after you retire. We share our sports and our lives with like-minded positive people. Most of them are very fit and inspire us to be the same. We can't stop the clock but we can sure have fun trying. I read two newspapers every day, a book a week, and keep abreast of things happening in the world. I am having a great life for which I am thankful every day.

My Advice

- Keep your brain active and alert.
- Have a positive attitude.
- Stay active.
- Watch your diet.

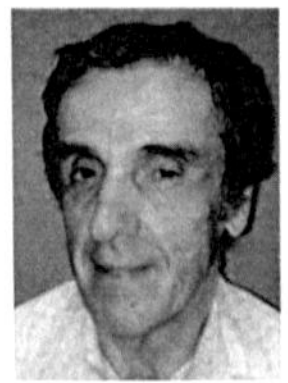

Name: Frank B.
Occupation: Hair Stylist, Business Owner
Retirement Age: Not Retired
Current Age: 75
Protirement Activities: **Not Retired**; **Health Enthusiast**

My Protirement

Back around 2000, I joined White Oaks Fitness Centre. I began spinning classes in the winter and cycling outside in the summer. I started resistance training and fine-tuned my nutrition to help with the cycling season. A club member suggested that I try yoga, so I tried it. It just about killed me at first, but I got through it and stayed with it because of its benefits.

I still enjoy working, so I expect I will continue working. I don't see any reason to stop. I may upgrade my hairstylist shop, may expand a bit, but there is no reason to stop.

My Advice

- No matter what your career, start and maintain a wellness program that is suited to you.
- Before retirement, start to improve your quality of life for after retirement.

CHAPTER 18: PROTIREMENT CATEGORY #14: LIFE LONG LEARNERS

"Anyone who stops learning is old, whether at 80 or 20. The greatest thing in life is to keep your mind young."
Henry Ford

Introduction

Significantly more Baby Boomers went to college and university than any previous generation. Learning became a norm for Boomers. This trend has continued throughout their lives and is now extending into the third chapter of their lives. Online education has made it even easier to learn a multitude of subjects. Many universities have free or discounted courses for seniors. There are also many adult education courses provided by non-profit organizations, recreation departments, senior centers, and other learning centers. The learning opportunities, both formal and informal, abound.

Facts about Lifelong Learners

Boomers who are active in paid or volunteer work are more involved in adult education. Participating, for personal interest reasons, becomes significant for those who are retired or reaching their retirement. Over 80 percent of adults over 65 state personal reasons drive their adult education decisions.

Education opportunities today are endless. Once the internet opened the door to learning, the opportunities multiplied exponentially. YouTube provides thousands of videos for individuals who want short concise overviews of a variety of topics.

In 2012, two Stanford Computer Science professors founded Coursera, an online 'classroom', to share knowledge and skills with the world.[27] Since then, they have built an online service where anyone can learn from professors and universities around world. There are 150 partner universities in 29 countries. Coursera offers over 2,000 courses covering almost every topic you can imagine. It is free to join Coursera, while the costs of courses range from $29 to $99.

"Lifelong Learners" Protirement Stories

I interviewed three people who engaged in Life Long Learning as a major Protirement activity. They ranged in age from 54 to 88.

"Lifelong Learners" personal Protirement Stories follow.

Name:	Lynn L.
Occupation:	Line Worker at GM
Retirement Age:	53
Current Age:	54
Protirement Activities:	**Life Long Learner;** Caregiver; Hobbyist; Health Enthusiast

My Protirement Story

It was awesome, retiring. I had no more shift work to worry about. Thirty-one years on the job was tiring. It was a very physical job. There were no more Sunday nights "fretting about having to go into work tomorrow." It was time. I just wanted to do something different. I went hot air ballooning and took guitar lessons. I am now a "rower mom" with my younger daughter. I also have more time to do quilting. Recently, I started kickboxing.

We see my parents, now, every Friday, when I take my mom to get her hair done, and every Sunday, when they come over for dinner. I also started working on a degree in Religion at the University of Waterloo.

It was very easy to stop working. I have not looked back once, but I miss some of the people and the social activities. I was able to be here for my husband when his mother died. I have also been able to be here more for our girls. My mom got sick so I have been able to help when needed. It's been positive not having the structure of shift work. Not having to rush is wonderful. Retiring was a positive experience.

I always worked on the assembly line or as a tool setter, mostly working with my hands and arms on the assembly line. Retiring was a lot better on my body and on my mind. Now, I am not rushed and that's the biggest thing I can say about retirement. I am not rushed! I don't have to rush to do anything anymore. I am more relaxed. You know, my only boss now is God, I don't have a supervisor or plant manager saying, "Lynn what are you doing?" There is nobody except for Him, and that is the best, just the best.

My Advice

- Give back to your community.
- Live independently.
- Follow your dreams, do what you want in retirement, as well as throughout your life. Don't wait for retirement to do those things, but rather continue them once retired.
- Live your life and be happy.
- Be kind.

Name: Maurice G.
Occupation: Banker
Retirement Age: 58
Current Age: 88
Protirement Activities: Contingency Worker; Hobbyist; **Travel Enthusiast; Community Builder;** Life Long Learner

My Protirement Story

I was 58 when I retired. It was not difficult making the transition from working for money to working for no money. I often say it was like getting off one merry-go-round and getting onto another. I have always had things to do. I never attended university, so after I retired I decided to start taking courses at Brock University. As a senior, I could audit courses for free. I took philosophy, astronomy, geology, history, and sociology. They have a swimming pool at the University, so I used it to get some exercise after class. Thus I was able to exercise both mind and body. I continued to take one course a year for six or seven years.

The area manager for Royal Bank asked me to be a Grey Panther. Grey Panthers were retirees who worked part-time for the Royal Bank helping people over 71 convert their retirement savings into Retirement Income Plans or annuities. As a Grey Panther I was able to work at times that were convenient to both me and the client, an ideal arrangement. I did that for six or seven years.

I was a volunteer with a non-profit children's mental health agency. For several years they talked about setting up a foundation So, when I finished being a Grey Panther I had a bit of spare time and agreed to take on the task of setting up a foundation. I recruited directors for the foundation board, obtained Letters Patent, got registration for Income Tax purposes, kept the minutes, prepared the agenda, prepared financial statements, solicited donations and issued receipts for Income Tax purposes. Gradually, we expanded the members on the foundation and eventually raised a million dollars.

I am a member of the Rotary Club, the Probus Club, and a member of a Probus Discussion Group. We meet monthly to solve the world problems! I am a member of the St. Catharines Historical Society, the Thorold Beaverdam Historical Society, the local branch of the Genealogical Society, the United Empire Loyalist Association, and an investment club. I audit the books for a couple of these associations.

I have been determining and recording the origin of the street names of St. Catharines. This is a project I hope to complete this year. The finished product will be turned over to the City of St. Catharines with the intention that it will be made available free of charge on their website to everyone who might be interested.

I sort the collection at church twice a month, and am a greeter at one service a month. I almost always have someone in a nursing home to visit. I do the house cleaning every Friday morning, and try to look after the grounds, but no longer have to cut the grass or shovel the snow, because my next door neighbor now insists on doing that for me. I bake our bread and prepare dinner once a week. Once a month I work at a community breakfast program for the needy. I play bridge about six times a month. Almost every day my wife and I play Faster Find, a word game requiring a certain amount of logic and concentration. So in this way we hope to stimulate our brains.

I try to keep myself in decent physical shape. I do Tai Chi every morning. It has become part of my regular routine. We have also done a fair amount of travelling. We have visited at least two dozen countries

I also do a fair amount of reading.

There is no one thing that takes up all my time, but put them all together and I have a fairly active life.

From the time I first retired, there was always something to do. The fact that I wasn't just sitting at home and wondering what to do made retirement an easy transition for both me and my wife.

I recently developed interest is opera, something I never thought would appeal to me. We see it on the big screen at a local cinema at the same time it is being seen at the Metropolitan Opera House in New York City. When you have the subtitles, see it on the big screen, with wonderful music, great acting and fantastic sets it is truly an enjoyable way to spend a Saturday afternoon.

As I age, I unfortunately have an increasing number of medical appointments and this eats up time, too.

My Advice

- Make having and maintaining a circle of friends a top priority.
- Do whatever you can to maintain your physical and mental well being.

- Remember, it is better to wear out than rust out.

Name:	Steve C.
Occupation:	Advertising Executive
Retirement Age:	Not Retired
Current Age:	66
Protirement Activities:	Seniorpreneur; **Life Long Learner**

My Protirement Story

I think you are dead when you stop learning. If you're not learning, nothing you do will be good enough to keep you going as you get older. I just think, at some point, the pressure of life and biology drains you of your life force or enthusiasm. If you don't love to learn, you will age faster. It's not so much learning how to be a wood worker or learning about quantum physics, but it's learning about what it is to be alive. I guess its humanity-based more than science-based. It's imaginative learning, expanding your imagination that's important. Your imagination shrinks like everything else, like every other muscle. If your imagination withers, that's what old is for us now. It's not really biological, it's more of an imaginative decline for me. For me, starting to love something now that is more internalized, like Shakespeare, is important. Stuff that moves the human essence higher than we normally reach is important.

We need to look above our pay grid in a way, to learn from people who are bigger, better, smarter, wiser, and more spiritually whole than we would normally be. If I ever did retire, I imagine I could play golf or go south or start wood working, but I would prefer to read Dante, read the bible, read Shakespeare, Dostoevsky; immerse myself in literature. A sideline while you were working and busy, like my reading, can become a focus in your protirement.

To me protirement is "pro" right now, it's not progressive, it's professional. We are the golden warriors of the economic life. We've been honing our skills and continually learning things. Protirement is where we are professionals. We've been doing it for 30 years. I think when you are 60, you may not know the latest

Snapchat gadget or Instagram filters, but in terms of moving business and seeing big picture, I think when you're 60, it doesn't mean you're old, it means you see things from high up. You're not stuck down in the early weeds of life, where everything is a tactic, you're way up here and you're seeing it all. That's what happens to us if we are any good at what we do.

My Advice

- Keep learning.
- Stretch your imagination.

CHAPTER 19: PROTIREMENT CATEGORY #15: PHILANTHROPISTS

"We make a living by what we get, but we make a life by what we give."
Winston Churchill

Introduction

Baby Boomers have always been a generation that supports charities through generous donations. This trend is continuing as Boomers age. There is a small group of Boomers who have chosen to set up their own focused funds, or funds within community foundations, agency foundations, university foundations, and other charitable organizations, to support causes that are close to their hearts. This is the group of Boomers that I call, the Philanthropists.

Facts about Philanthropists

Boomers have always supported charitable causes and this is continuing as they age. They support a wide range of causes, including: social service charities, United Way, health organizations, children's charities, educational institutions, homeless programs, mental health agencies, hospitals, food banks, multi-cultural programs, recreational activities, human rights causes, environmental causes, cultural programs, religious institutions, international programs, and more.

Over the past 20 years, community foundations have become a common way of facilitating giving at a community level across North America. They are independently registered foundations that act as grant-making foundations; have a broad goal of improving the quality of life in a specific community; are supported by a broad range of private and public donors; are governed by individuals who represent the community; and build endowment funds which contribute to their sustainability. Individuals, families, organizations, and businesses are setting up individual endowment funds within a community foundation through which they can direct their individual giving to support community initiatives. The uniqueness of a community foundation is the pooling of all the funds for investment purposes.

Boomers are also large donors to universities and hospitals, which have sophisticated donor programs. Universities have a wide variety of funds to which people can donate, including initiatives like scholarship funds, building funds, departmental alumni funds, sports programs, and research chairs. Hospitals have building campaigns, equipment campaigns, and research campaigns.

Some individuals establish their own family foundations to personally direct their giving during their Protirement. These foundations focus on issues that are of interest to the individual families. Interests can vary significantly, including: health, social issues, environment, religion, arts, education, community building, etc.

"Philanthropists" Protirement Stories

I interviewed two individuals who were Philanthropists in the Protirement and have directed their personal giving through the establishment of different types of funds or foundations. They were 71 and 80 years old.

"Philanthropists" personal Protirement Stories follow.

Name: Sharron R.
Occupation: Social Worker
Retirement Age: 65
Current Age: 71
Protirement Activities: Hobbyist; Travel Enthusiast; Community Builder; Health Enthusiast; **Philanthropist; Family Enthusiast**

My Protirement Story

It wasn't an adjustment at all when I retired. I loved my job but was tired of the stresses associated with working and wanted time for myself. There were projects that I was committed to while working that I've continued with as a volunteer. It is six years later and I am still involved in some of them. I signed up as a volunteer with the agency before I even left it.

My partner and I have also travelled, taking a number of small trips as well as a couple of big ones to Africa, Antarctica and Greenland and the Northwest Passage. We visit regularly with family in Quebec and I spend most of the summer at our cottage in Nova Scotia. My partner's nephew in Quebec has a son who is an avid hockey player, which allows us to go to hockey tournaments there. We could have done it while working, but it allows us to go and not have to rush back on Sunday night for work on Monday. He's like our grandson and we are fortunate in that we can support his dream to be the best hockey player he can be and see where it takes him.

We go to numerous music concerts and film festivals. We've done some major work in the house and are planning to renovate the attic. Weather permitting, we spend a lot of time in our garden.

When I turned 60, we used money donated for my birthday to establish "Sharron & Mary's Way Cool Kids, Roots and Wings Fund" at the Children's Aid Society (CAS) Foundation. The fund gives money to current & former youth in the care of CAS Toronto to help them connect with their roots (culture, ethnicity, religion, race, sexual orientation and gender identity and expression) and to discover & spread their wings (dreams, aspirations, memories or talents). Often the Fund is used when there is no other source of funding. Some examples of what we fund are: a couple of youth who needed to get their beloved cats fixed in order to keep them with them in their housing; tickets for a youth, who was really into music, to go to a concert that was important to him; a youth needing to buy a horse in order to be accepted into a prestigious equine school which helped change her life course; helping a young man have dentistry for badly formed teeth that caused him to be bullied, affecting his self-confidence; helping to send a young Mom to Africa so she could introduce her baby to their relatives; and helping a youth go through the transition from female to male.

I joined a gym, which I go to a couple of times a week. I keep very active. My plan to spend all day sitting at home reading books and the paper day has mostly gone out the window- although I read the paper and do the crossword every day. We attend interesting lectures and other community events. We joined CARP to know about things that are going on and relevant to seniors. We took on the lead role in re-establishing the Toronto CAS Staff Alumni which is just pure fun. We have a planning committee of about 10 people, meet at a local pub, and when not reminiscing and laughing, plan events for our fellow Alumni. As you can see, we are involved in many different fun activities that keep us busy all the time.

My Advice

- Get involved in community activities, of which there are many regardless of where you live.
- Develop interests other than work long before you retire. Don't be stuck when you're 65 thinking your whole life involves your work, all your friends are from work and all your interests are connected to work. While important, work should only be one aspect of one's life. View retirement as an opportunity to do all those things you never had time to do while working.
- In this age of technology, when so many people relate through machines, make time for personal face-to-face relationships. Spend time with your family, friends and neighbors.
- Make time for young people in your life. They provide you with interesting and thought provoking perspectives on life and the world that help keep you current. Their energy is

boundless and infectious, and they're fun to be with. They will be generous with their help and support and in return you can share your personal history, experience and wisdom from which they can learn and benefit. It's a win-win experience.

Name: Terry O'Malley
Occupation: CEO, Advertizing Firm
Retirement Age: 66
Current Age: 80
Protirement Activities: **Corporate Side Hustles;** Community Builder; Health Enthusiast; **Philanthropist;** Political Activist; Family Enthusiast

My Protirement Story

I retired from the marketing world when I was 66. My key to post retirement was to have some kind of discipline. I got my own office; having an office gives me discipline. I come in every day around 10 or 10:30 and stay until about 1:00.

I took some money out of my savings to invest. If it makes money or loses money, it doesn't matter. I became a major shareholder of a baseball team in Niagara. My mentor was Senator Keith Davey who opened every door imaginable for me. He put me together with other investors who were able to buy the team from the Blue Jays. That was my first investment. We had the team for five years and then sold it to the New York Mets.

With the profits from the sale, I bought a condo in Florida, which I still have. We tried to re-launch the Taylor and Bate Brewery here but it didn't work out. We tried to launch a TV station in Niagara in 2001, but couldn't get a license. We tried again in 2010, were able to get a license, but weren't able to get the investors that time. With a group of 20 partners, we bought the Ottawa Lacrosse Team and moved it to Toronto. We renamed it the Toronto Rock Lacrosse Team. We eventually sold the team.

My other love is Harvard, which has been my weapon. I developed a scholarship at Harvard in my name for a St.

Catharines student who had high grades and was well rounded but needed financial assistance. If there wasn't a St. Catharines student then it would open to Niagara, and then, if necessary, to Ontario.

I also opened two scholarships at Niagara College in honor of Senator Davey, my mentor. This is what makes it all worthwhile, receiving hand written thank you notes from the recipients of the scholarships.

Through it all, I had this commitment to fitness. I work out every day. I went 31 years and 77 days doing the equivalent of a 10k run. I still do two hours a day. I call it my daily vacation. I am able to sort things out, it's just part of my life.

I became involved at Brock University and was on the board and the President's Council. I started a lecture series on advertizing and marketing at Brock 15 years ago. The university's president calls it a signature event and I am very proud of that. I have been a mentor to some of the students who participated in this series and love the mentoring role.

I have also been very involved in politics. I have worked on many election campaigns over the years, beginning with Phil Givens' mayoral campaign for the City of Toronto, and working on campaigns for Mitchell Sharpe, Pierre Trudeau, John Turner, Jean Chretien, David Peterson, Art Eggleton, and Justin Trudeau.

My Advice

- Stay active.
- Find something that really interests you and do it.
- Have some discipline and routine in your life.
- Stay in contact with people.
- Enjoy your grandchildren.

CHAPTER 20: PROTIREMENT CATEGORY #16: FAMILY ENTHUSIASTS

"Family is not an important thing, it's everything."
Michael J. Fox

Introduction

Over a third of the people interviewed referred to the importance of keeping in touch with family post-retirement. People talked about how significant it was to maintain contact with their children, grandchildren, extended family, and their partners. Their Protirement stories, and the Advice section, are filled with anecdotes about how much they have come to value family during their later years. The greatest focus of family time, and subsequent joy, was spending time with grandchildren.

It is important to note that I only identified 'Family Enthusiasts' as a Protirement Activity for those who talked about spending time with family, or gave advice about the importance of spending time with family, during their interviews. This is a unique Protirement Activity. I believe many of those interviewed talked about other Protirement activities without mentioning family activities because it was just 'something they did as part of life'. Therefore, many individuals would probably agree that they are 'Family Enthusiasts', even though they have not been identified as so in their stories.

Facts about Family Enthusiasts

In my research, I found some interesting facts related to family, as they relate to the importance of grand parenting, the most frequently mentioned family activity during retirement.

In 2016, the American Grandparents Association published the results of a survey titled, Surprising Facts about Grandparents[28]. Some facts include:

- 72% think being a grandparent is the single most important and satisfying thing in their life;
- 63% say they can do a better job caring for grandchildren than they did with their own children;
- 68% think being a grandparent brings them closer to their adult children;
- 90% enjoy talking about their grandkids to whomever will listen.

According to this survey, the profile of grandparents is changing:

- 43% became grandparents in their fifties;
- By 2010, more than 50% of the grandparent population were Baby Boomers; by 2015 it had increased to almost 60%.
- Grandparents are able to relate to their grandkids because they are also wired:
- 73% are online;
- 70% use search engines;
- 63% shop online;
- 30% instant message/text;
- 56% share photos online;
- 46% bank online; and
- 45% are on social networks like Facebook, Instagram, and Twitter.

"Family Enthusiasts" Protirement Stories

Thirty-five people talked about the importance of family during their retirement. Twenty-four of these individuals talked about family during their interviews; four mentioned the importance of family while sharing Advice, and seven referred to family both during their Protirement Stories and while sharing Advice.

Three of those individuals are highlighted under "Family Enthusiasts" while the others are referred to under other Protirement Activities. Those in this section range in age from 69 to 80.

Grand parenting, as highlighted above, was clearly the most frequently mentioned 'family' involvement. Examples of comments include:

- Bonnie talked about staying close to your family; "It's such a source of joy, being around grandchildren, never underestimate it."
- Peter talked about settling in Ottawa "as our base closer their son and his family. Grand parenting is a joy and we will be bouncing from Ottawa, where we will have soon have two grandchildren, and Whistler where we have one."
- Robin described: "focus on grandkids, with babysitting, support to parents, and visiting to be with them, travel with them, and learning with them."
- Gil talked about his grandchildren and their impact on his decisions; "One of my granddaughters is now the University of Nevada about 20 miles from where we live now. Our children are starting to get grey hair, and our grandchildren are getting to be adult age. I think my wife is probably right; I am getting ready to transition to the next stage, which will be much more family focused, trying to leave a legacy for the future."
- David has 12 grandchildren. "Family, to me, is extremely important."
- John stressed that: "Family is critical."
- Maureen thought it was important to: "Make sure family focus stays paramount while you are working, so it will be there after you retire."

"Family Enthusiasts" personal Protirement Stories follow:

Name: Jagdishchandra A.M.
Occupation: Physician
Retirement Age: 65
Current Age: 80
Protirement Activities: New Careers/Jobs; **Travel Enthusiast;** Community Builder; Health Enthusiast; **Family Enthusiast**

My Protirement Story

When I retired from the Shaver Hospital as Medical Director, I had a part-time consulting practice in Niagara Falls and Welland. I served as a volunteer Medical Director of the Lung Association in Welland.

It was very difficult to just bring the curtain down and retire completely. So, I started to do two things: working less hours and taking longer vacations. I was fortunate because I had a house in Mumbai that we lived in for three or four months a year. I was just lucky that I had very efficient secretary who stayed with me as I reduced my practice. I go to Rotary meetings when I am in India and travelling. Rotary has been a major part of my life as I am a Rotarian for more than three decades.

In September 2012, I decided that I was going to retire completely.

I decided that once I retired, I would not be involved in any medical practice. I gave away my license and everything related to it. In the mornings, we go for a work-out and then come back and have breakfast. Then I go on the computer and look at how my investments are doing and what else is happening in the world. Then, after lunch, I have a nap and then have tea. If my wife wants to go shopping I'll take her shopping. I spend about 1-2 hours reading. And spend time with friends socializing.

We travel to different parts of the world. I'm out of the country for three or four months a year. We take the cruises to different parts of the world. Three years ago, we went to Paris and then took a train to Amsterdam. From there we took a boat to Russia.

I read and spend time with my grandchildren.

The biggest problem in retirement, if you have no money issues or health issues, you have to be very careful that you are spending, in a close environment, 24 hours a day with your wife. It was an adjustment for me. I would advise everybody that when you are thinking about you're going to retire, make sure that you have taken this into consideration.

My Advice

- Your health is a life-long maintenance activity, stay healthy.
- Manage your finances with professional help and keep your wife and children informed about your will and finances. Make sure all your paper work is done properly with professional help so that your loved ones-survivors
- are not confused and frustrated.
- You have to have family and friends in your life.
- Be aware of the adjustment involved in suddenly spending 24/7 with your partner after you retire.
- Finally try to find out what makes you and your loved ones happy.

Name:	Lynda B.
Occupation:	GM Administration, Material Control/ Traffic
Retirement Age:	54
Current Age:	69
Protirement Activities:	**New Career/Job;** Seniorpreneur; Caregiver; Hobbyist; Travel Enthusiast; **Family Enthusiast**

My Protirement Story

In October 2001, I retired from General Motors after 34 years of service in the Traffic & Material Control Departments. Many friendships were formed during my career and several lasting through the years.

In the Spring of 2002, my friend and I started a business called Gardening Angels which is gardening in the cemetery. After being in the office for so many years we were looking for an opportunity to work outside and give back to the community. As part of our plan we involved the Brain Injury Association. Since inception, the company has continued to grow and eventually the Brain Injury Association purchased the business and currently have over 300 sites which they service. I am very proud of this endeavor.

In the meantime I won a prize which entitled me to a one year membership at White Oaks for their gym. During this time, I was offered a job at the front desk of the Club and have now been there for over 10 years. I enjoy the members and all the friendships that have flourished.

I also have a Grandson who is eight years old and who is always fun to be around. He is involved in swimming and baseball during the summer months and we are always present at these events to cheer him on. Also, I have a Mom who will be 95 this year and has dementia. She lives in a nursing home close to our home so we visit as much as possible.

My husband and I love to travel and have been fortunate enough to visit a lot of the European countries plus Australia/New Zealand and Hawaii over the years. Most recently we have taken two months of the winter and vacation in Palm Desert, California.

My Advice

- Keep active
- Find something you really enjoy doing outside of work, it may be something that is totally different that you've done before
- Keep your mind busy and occupied
- Have a purpose in life
- Keep involved with family, friends, life is too short
- Join a group or volunteer

Name:	Dr. Robin W.
Occupation:	Pediatrician, Medical Officer of Health
Retirement Age:	65
Current Age:	71
Protirement Activities:	**New Career/Job;** Travel Enthusiast; **Family Enthusiast**

My Protirement Story

After I retired from my position as Medical Officer of Health for a Public Health Department the Province of Ontario, being extremely short handed, called me in February and asked if I would consider doing a 1 year extension with them, as an Associate Chief Medical Officer of Health. We considered it while on vacation in Hawaii for two weeks. We thought it would be okay. We loved Toronto, my husband had family there, and we love art, music and the symphony. It felt like it could be an interesting year. So we rented a condo in downtown Toronto. At the same time we sold our family home here in Niagara and built this home. The contract extended to a year and a half, then I went back for three months, and the summer before I worked for the entire summer, and then I went back two days a week as an ACMOH until this past December. Since then, I have been doing a specific project for the Ministry related to drug monitoring.

I am interested in people, cooking, and go to Chautauqua regularly.

There is lots of support of the family and friends at this time in their lives. I am pretty good on the food, the help, the nursing, while my husband is pretty good on the intellectual and emotional support. It's not an organized thing, it comes and goes and you do it when you're needed. In terms of giving back and feeling worthwhile, there is always focus on grandkids, with babysitting support to parents and visiting to be with them, travel with them, and learning with them.

We watch a lot of films and go to the Shaw plays. I golf as much as I can squeeze it in.

My Advice

- Think a little bit about it before your retire.
- Think about the things that give you value beyond your profession, your work.
- Keep active and well.
- Choose to be curious.

CHAPTER 21: PROTIREMENT CATEGORY #17: LIFE ENTHUSIASTS

"The purpose of life, after all, is to live it, to taste experience to the utmost, to reach out eagerly and without fear for newer and richer experience."
Eleanor Roosevelt

Introduction

I interviewed 100 people for this book. Most of them had clear preferences among their Protirement activities. Almost everyone had both primary Protirement activities, where they focused much of their energy, and secondary Protirement activities, where they focused less of their energy. A smaller group loved to get involved in many different Protirement activities without focusing on any one or two. They reminded me of people who love buffet restaurants where they can sample a bit of everything. In the same way, Life Enthusiasts love to sample a buffet of Protirement activities without getting over involved in any one or two.

Facts about Life Enthusiasts

There is little research on this particular group. My Life Enthusiasts included a chemical lab researcher, a not-for-profit human resources executive, an automotive quality resources technician, and an administrator in an automotive dealership. They come from very different backgrounds and enjoy very different Protirement activities. The one commonality is that they all enjoy many Protirement activities without specializing in any single one.

"Life Enthusiasts" Protirement Stories

I interviewed four Life Enthusiasts. They range in age from 58 to 79.

"Life Enthusiasts" personal Protirement Stories follow.

Name:	Ben C.
Occupation:	Chemical Research & Development Technician
Retirement Age:	55
Current Age:	73
Protirement Activities:	**Life Enthusiast**

My Protirement Story

Although I never went to university, I listen to TED Talks a lot and love learning from them.

I have always had hobbies. I played golf for many years, learned to wind surf, ran marathons, played tennis and badminton, and learned martial arts. We have travelled to China, Europe, and Hawaii. We are a member of a dinner club and have a social group that meet regularly for dinners. I paint, have an aquarium, and love doing home renovations.

My Advice

- You have to be nice to others; people will forget anything except how you make them feel.
- T.T.T. "Things Take Time." Don't be afraid to try new things; ask for help to learn new hobbies, sports, etc.
- Don't buy anything before you try it. Don't own it, but operate it for enough time to really see if you want to buy it.

Name: Maureen C.
Occupation: Human Resources Director, Non-Profit
Retirement Age: 61
Current Age: 64
Protirement Activities: **Life Enthusiast**

My Protirement Story

When I had the opportunity to become director, it changed my retirement plans. Originally, my plan was to have a year at home alone before my husband retired. I had never been home alone. My husband had two year-long sabbaticals during his career, so he had experience being home alone without work commitments. But then the director position became available. That changed my plans and I gave a commitment of three years, but stayed for five years, during which time my husband retired.

For a year, my boss knew I was planning on leaving. I wanted to choose a meaningful date to leave. My boss had chosen my birthday for her retirement day, so I chose my late mother's birthday for *my* retirement day.

I know myself well enough to know that I need structure, so that influenced my planning for retirement. I needed some kind of cornerstone. I usually went to the gym at night, after work. I went to the gym my first day of retirement in the morning, and never looked back. I come home at 11:00 or 11:30 and shower. By then, it's lunch time. I had 400 lunch dates the first year after my retirement. I didn't want to schedule myself too much, so we went to Florida and did some travelling. A close friend lost her husband, so I was able to spend some time with her. We travelled whenever we wanted instead of only during the summer.

I thought I might do some volunteer or contract work like mediation or harassment investigations, but I quickly ruled them all out. I had worked in conflictual situations most of my career, trying to resolve them, and I felt that I had enough of that. I'm a very "glass is half full" person and didn't want to deal with the "shit" any more. I didn't want to deal with complainers anymore. To the best of my ability, I wanted to deal with the good stuff in my retirement.

I didn't do any volunteer work, either. I met this group of women that I play Mahjong with once a week. I enjoy the competition. I also go to the gym six mornings a week. That's my structure, and everything else is "as I go along."

Both of my boys are engaged and I am being introduced to two new families, so I am spending time on that right now. I also recently had a grandson. I was ready for a grandson, so it's all good. Now, I have a new structure where we'll be seeing our kids and grandson at least every month, whether we go to Toronto, where they live, or they come here to Montreal.

When I was planning to retire, my husband used to say, "Maureen, you are always the expert at work everyone goes to for answers. What are you going to do when no one comes to ask you questions?" I always coached people to leave when they were at their best, so it was a good time to go. As I said before, I play Mahjong with a group of women. I was always good at math, so I was the quickest to catch on with the game and I am the "go to" person when anyone has a question. We all learn together, but when the person who taught us isn't there, and she only visits periodically, they always ask me the questions. So it re-emerges in different ways. I am still the person people go to with questions; it's just different questions, so I don't mind.

My Advice

- Maintain a healthy work-life balance.
- Make sure leisure time stays important while you are working so it will continue once you retire.
- Make sure family focus stays important while you are working so it will be there after you retire.

Name:	Noreen C.
Occupation:	GM Line Tool Setter, Machinist, Quality Resource Technician
Retirement Age:	55
Current Age:	58
Protirement Activities:	**Life Enthusiast**

My Protirement Story

I was ready to retire when I was 55. I went into work one day and, at a meeting, signed the papers. After that, I picked up the phone and called my husband and told him I was retiring in a few months. I loved my job, I loved the people, everything about it, but I didn't want to work anymore. I was tired of working. I wanted "me" time. As well, my mother got sick. I was going to volunteer at a nursing home, but never did, because my mom needed me and I wanted to be available. Sometimes, I take her to doctor appointments, help with the cooking, or any other things they need help with. My sisters and I, we all pitch in.

Friends from work get together for lunches and suppers once in a while, and we just did a paint night. I joined gym, the best thing I ever did for myself, and I love it. It's a Boot Camp. It's a social place for me. After Boot Camp, we sometimes go for breakfast. We have different things that we do together.

As a woman, I never get bored. In the winter, I need to do something. We go away for the month of February, I never get bored in the summer, but come the winter time, I get restless. I like having "me" time. I go to the gym, go shopping, bake, get my nails done, and go for lunch with my friends. I am never tired. I feel better now than in my whole life. I volunteer for the rowing in Welland. I don't want to commit to something when I have to be available at set times. I love that I can go to Toronto when I want to visit my sister. We go shopping together, spend time at her house. We travel a couple of times each year.

My Advice

- Need to really make sure that you are ready to retire.
- Have to have the mind set for retiring.
- Have no regrets.
- Have to maintain your friendships.

Name:	Patti H.
Occupation:	Automobile Dealership Administration
Retirement Age:	45
Current Age:	79
Protirement Activities:	**Life Enthusiast**

My Protirement Story

I joined White Oaks and played racquet ball and tennis, and did more skiing with the girls. I met a lot of nice people. I lived in the Clusters, which was the main condominium in St, Catharines at the time. It was party central, and being the only single at the time, I was often the party convenor.

I did a lot of travelling. Five years later, I met John, my current partner. Our 30th anniversary is coming up this November. Today, I keep busy with my grandchildren, gardening, and caring for my husband.

My Advice

- Keep active.
- Stay active, both physically and mentally.
- Do some volunteer work in the community.

CHAPTER 22: PROTIREMENT, NOT RETIREMENT

"If you believe in it, and
can commit to it –
***do it!*"**
Pamela Minns

Introduction

I began my interviews with a curiosity about what people were doing in their retirement years. I quickly learned that retirement has evolved for the Baby Boomer generation. I wanted to better understand what Boomers were doing in their retirement, how they were spending their time, what challenges they had in adjusting to retirement, and what advice they had for others who had not yet retired.

Retirement is Not a Destination

As I interviewed people, I began to realize that retirement was no longer a destination Boomers strived to reach. Boomers' grandparents and earlier generations worked until they could no longer work, and then they retired. They spent their retired life at home with family, recognizing that there were only a few years to live for most of them. The retirement industry did not exist for these earlier generations. It was only with Boomers' parents that a retirement industry began to develop. Retirement communities in warmer climates began to grow in popularity; airfare began to decrease in cost, promoting tourism among retirees; golf became a big retirement activity, and private pension plans and government pensions made it easier to retire and still actively participate in life. But life spans were still shorter than they are today.

Fast forward to the Boomer generation and life spans have grown significantly thanks to advancements in medicine and health promotion activities. Boomers realize that they could live almost a third of their lives after they retire. As a result, the first wave of Boomers has reinvented the retirement concept. Boomers reject the label of "retired" and want to stay engaged with life. Rather than retirement being a destination, or end of the road, it has become the first step in a journey to find new meaning in the third chapter of their lives.

Life 3.0 describes a generational change in how Boomers are approaching retirement. I identified this change through interviews with 100 Baby Boomers and pre-Boomers. As a result of an analysis of these interviews, I identified a three-stage process people were going through once they decided it was time to retire. This three-stage process has evolved out of Boomers' desire to get more out of the third chapter of their lives.

Summary

Stage 1 is the Retirement Stage. Boomers experience a range of emotions including sadness, disorientation, uncertainty, a sense of loss and excitement. Stage 2 is the Transition Zone. Faced with a lack of routine, loss of social status, loss of identity, and loss of socializing, Boomers engage in transitional projects and begin dealing with the transitional issues in life, creating new routines, new identities, and exploring new socializing opportunities. Completing a Personal Inventory also assists with the transition and exploration of new activities. Stage 3, the Protirement Stage, is where Boomers begin to engage in new Protirement activities. They also create new daily routines, develop a new sense of self, a new social status, and often new friendships as a result of their protirement activities.

I identified 17 Protirement Categories of activities that Boomers were engaged in, and developed the *Protirement Checkerboard* to summarize these activities.

Protirement Checkerboard

Not Retired/ Gradually Retiring	Contingency Workers	New Careers/Jobs	Seniorpreneurs
Caregivers	Political Activists	Hobbyists	Corporate Side Hustles
Travel Enthusiasts	Community Builders	Socializers	Writers/ Performers
Health Enthusiasts	Life Long Learners	Philanthropists	Family Enthusiasts

Life Enthusiasts

The most surprising thing I learned from my interviewees and research was that many Baby Boomers are not ready to completely retire from the work force. Although financial reasons are partially responsible for this trend, lifestyle reasons are just as important. The non-financial reasons that underlay Baby Boomers desire to work into the third chapter of their lives include the reality that work provides:

- them with a purpose;
- a sense of identity;
- an increase in self-worth;
- a routine and structure to daily life;
- intellectual stimulation; and
- social interaction.

The first four Protirement Categories on the Checkerboard are work-related Protirement Categories. The remaining 13 Categories are non-work Protirement activities.

Baby Boomers are multi-taskers. Boomers are often engaged in a number of these Protirement activities at the same time. Boomers have primary and secondary Protirement activities, where they chose to spend greater and lesser amounts of time. Many Boomers are involved in two, three—and more—Protirement activities at any given time.

When I completed work on the Protirement Checkerboard, I mapped out my personal Checkerboard and found that I fit well into the description of the multi-tasker. My primary Protirement activities, highlighted in italics below, include: Seniorpreneurs, Community Builders, and Writers/Performers. My secondary Protirement activities, not italicized, include: Hobbyists, Travel Enthusiasts, and Health Enthusiasts.

Ellis Katsof's Protirement Checkerboard

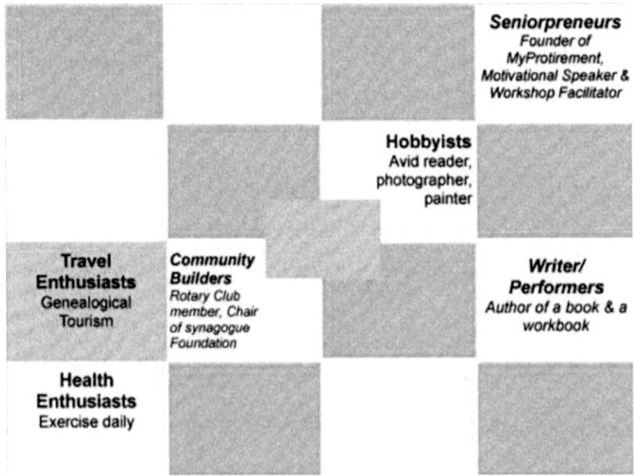

The Protirement Checkerboard provides Boomers with a template to begin exploring fulfilling activities during the third chapter of their lives. The Checkerboard is meant to be an evolving expression of our activities as we journey through Protirement. Boomers are regularly adding and dropping activities from their Protirement Checkerboard as they journey through their Protirement years.

Much advice has been given by the people interviewed. They were keen on providing readers with advice based on their experiences. The pre-Protirement advice that stands out in my mind is the importance of staying engaged in non-work activities *while* we are working. As easy as this sounds, it is difficult for many of us to do because the challenging nature of our work in the later stages of our careers. People stressed the importance of being engaged in some non-work activities that can become the initial foundation of Protirement life that we can build on as we begin the journey from retirement to Protirement.

Physical health, mental wellness, and brain health were continuous themes in the Protirement advice section. People were very aware of the impact that our overall health will have on our Protirement journey. Although there are health challenges that we cannot prevent, there are many that can be avoided with a healthy lifestyle. People focused on physical activity, nutrition, mental wellness, and brain activity as being crucial for an enhanced Protirement lifestyle.

Final Thoughts

Boomers really dislike the term "retirement." It has taken on a stigma of 'giving up on life', 'being over the hill', and 'being redundant'. Boomers do not feel any of these things and do not live life with these beliefs. Therefore, I strongly believe that it is time for us to begin using the term 'retirement' as only the first stage in a process of redefining our lives after we retire or turn 65. The term 'Protirement' has become common place in Australia and the UK, and it is time for us to adopt the term in North America. It is time for us to begin using the term 'Protirement' and creating exciting, vibrant Protirement lifestyles.

INDEX

1. Bright Paper, (Sun Life Assurance Company of Canada, February, 2013), 2.
2. Wiktionary.org, https://en.wiktionary.org/wiki/protirement
3. William Bridges, *"Managing Transitions: Making the Most of Change",* https://wmbridges.com/what-is-transition
4. Louise Penny, *The Nature of the Beast*, (Minotaur Books, 2015), 53
5. Charles Handy, *The Second Curve, Thoughts no Reinventing Society* (Penguin Random House, 2015), 23
6. "Reinventing Retirement – The Boomers Are Not All Retiring 'On Schedule'" (Zoomer Media, November 9, 2012)
7. Mark Miller, "Take This Job and Love It!" (AARP Magazine, February/March 2015) http://www.aarp.org/work/working-after-retirement/info-2015/work-over-retirement-happiness.html
8. Ibid
9. "Majority of Canadians Feel They Can't Afford to Retire", (The Conference Board of Canada, 2014)
10. Russell Heimlich, "Baby Boomers Retire", (Pew Research Center, Fact Tank News in the Numbers, December 29, 2010)
11. CIBC Poll: Short on Savings, Canada's 50-Somethings plan to retire at age 63 - and keep working, (CIBC, August 20, 2012)
12. Helaine Olen, "You Call This Retirement? Boomers Still Have Work to Do", (AARP The Magazine, July 2016)
13. David Nilssen, "You Call This Retirement? Boomers Still Have Work to Do", (Entrepreneur, October 30, 2015)

14. Statistics Canada, “Bridge Employment”, http://www.statcan.gc.ca/pub/75-001-x/2008111/article/10719-eng.htm#a1
15. Benjamin Tal, “Start-ups – Present and Future” (CIBC, September 25, 2012) http://research.cibcwm.com/economic_public/download/if_2012-0925.pdf
16. Paull Webe, Michael Schaper, “Understanding the Grey Entrepreneur: A Review of the Literature” (2014) https://www.researchgate.net/publication/228790393_Understanding_the_Grey_Entrepreneur_A_review_of_the_Literature
17. Robert W. Fairlie, Arnobio Morelix, E.J. Reedy, Joshua Russell, “2015 The Kauffman Index Startup Activity National Trends” (The Kauffman Foundation, 2015)
18. Joe Wasylyk, “Encore! Encore!” (Joe Wasylyk, 2014), 8
19. Dr. Ruth Williams, “Seniorpreneur: We Need You” (University of Melbourne, March, 2016)
20. “Portrait of Caregivers” (Statistics Canada, 2012) Table 1, Number and proportion of caregivers, by characteristics of caregivers
21. Ryan Deska, “Municipal Councillor Profile” (Rural Ontario Institute), 17
22. Wikipedia, https://en.wikipedia.org/wiki/List_of_hobbies
23. Ontario Blue Cross, https://on.bluecross.ca/travel-insurance/travel-tips/518-baby-boomer-travel-trends
24. Volunteer Canada, “Data on Giving, Volunteering and Participating in Canada, 2013, https://volunteer.ca/gvp
25. Volunteer Canada, https://volunteer.ca/content/new-digital-tool-classifies-canadians-according-six-volunteer-types-and-suggests-suitable
26. Alex Brain, *Just Breathe* http://justbreathemag.com/life/holistic-lifestyle/9-benefits-of-socializing/
27. Coursera, https://www.coursera.org
28. American Grandparents Association, “Surprising Facts About Grandparents”, http://www.grandparents.com/food-and-leisure/did-you-know/surprising-facts-about-grandparents

ABOUT THE AUTHOR: ELLIS KATSOF

Ellis is founder and CEO of *My*Protirement, a business focused on changing people's attitudes toward retirement. Ellis is a motivational speaker, workshop facilitator and consultant on Protirement and the development of exciting, personalized Protirement Lifestyle Plans. His book, *Life 3.0,* explores Protirement through the eyes of 100 retired North Americans from all walks of life, whom Ellis has personally interviewed. They include financial analysts, automotive assembly workers, teachers, lawyers, wealth management advisors, doctors, politicians, athletes, musicians, spiritual leaders, a newspaper publisher, coal miner, fire fighter/Captain, administrative assistants, psychologists, a sociologist, and more.

Ellis has designed the "Protirement Checkerboard," which introduces 17 distinct Protirement activities that Baby Boomers are engaging in, including four Bridge Employment activities.

Prior to launching *My*Protirement, Ellis was a highly-accomplished leader in the not-for-profit and public sector, with over 36 years of experience. After graduating with his MSW, Ellis worked in the non-profit sector, and for provincial and regional governments. He then began his consulting career, and for six years, consulted in both the non-profit and for profit sectors.

Ellis is a Fellow of the Ivey Business School CommunityShift Program; a graduate of the Schulich School of Business/CODI Organization Development Program; and a recipient of the Brand Foundation Coaching Scholarship for individuals who exhibit innovative leadership.

Ellis has been a Rotarian since 2005, and has been recognized as a Paul Harris Fellow.